For Maria,
May our faithfulness
to God be in tune

Faithfully Yours

with God's wonderful

A Collection of Messages for Christian Women

faithfulness to us!

God Bless you,
Judy Miller
Prov. 3:5,6.

Faithfully Yours

A Collection of Messages for Christian Women

Judy Miller and Farris Parker

Dawn Publications
2103 N. Memorial Court
Pasadena, Texas 77502

Faithfully Yours
A Collection of Messages for Christian Women

DEDICATION

To Jule and Hack

Without whose love, faith and encouragement we could not have completed this endeavor.

Contents

ACKNOWLEDGMENTS

Fairy and I began thinking about compiling this book one night as we visited after Sunday evening services. As teachers of Ladies' Bible Classes, we have a desire to share our messages beyond the local classrooms.

Our warm appreciation is given to the following for permission to use parts of their work in our book:

Joe Barnett ... Quotation on page 26,

Donna Horne ... Quotation on page 66, from *Meanwhile, Back in the Jungle.* Published by J. C. Choate Publications, Winona, MI 38967.

Ruby Jones ... Quotation on page 29, from her column entitled "ODDS 'N' ENDS." Daleville, Indiana 47334.

Ethelyn Mitchell ... Quotation on page 61. From *Come Unto Me,* Published by Quality Printing Co., Inc. Abilene, TX Copyright 1963.

Two of my favorite poets have contributed to our book. For their expressions of beauty and gracious permission to use their poems, we are deeply grateful.

Gifted with rare insight and always perceptive, Mary Oler's poem "If You Could Have Another Life" lifts our spirits. This poem is taken from Mary's collection of poetry entitled *A Bit of America,* printed by JUST A MOMENT COMPANY, Quinlan, Texas.

Beauty, joy and wonder are always captured in Garnett Ann Schultz's lovely poems. We are especially grateful that she has allowed us to use two of her poems, "The Test" and "I Know" from her books *Moments of Sunshine* and *To Touch a Star,* both published by Dorrance and Company, Philadelphia.

Fairy and I also want to thank our individual Ladies' Bible Classes for their encouragement and faith in us.

A great big thanks goes to Mary Nell Hasty for editing our manuscript and writing the Foreword.

A personal note from Farris:

My part in this book would not have been possible had it not been for Jule and Judy Miller. Brother Miller's suggestions and editing are very much appreciated.

Both Farris (Fairy) and Jule have been an inspiration to me. Fairy waited patiently for me to complete my part and, I, as ever, turned to my husband Jule for strength and love, as well as his excellent editing ability.

— Judy Miller

FOREWORD

For the past twelve years I have been privileged to know Judy Miller and Fairy Parker. I have sat in their classes and gained understanding of spiritual things from their teaching. I have worked on projects with them and admired their dedication to the Lord and His church. I have spent hours of quiet friendship with them and learned about love.

You can be assured that the words in this book come from hearts completely committed to knowing God and serving Him and His people. It was written by women who are—Faithfully His.

— *Mary Nell Hasty*

Introduction

Faithfully Yours is a "potpourri" of subjects dealing in a practical manner with topics of interest to women of all ages.

This book is co-authored by Judy Miller and Farris Parker. It is designed to be used as a class book for ladies, a personal study guide or inspirational reading.

Judy and Farris have been friends for many years and have long wanted to collaborate their efforts into one work. Each writer has drawn from years of experience as a Bible teacher and lecturer.

This joint effort is meant to inspire other women to study, to teach, to serve and live faithfully giving God the glory.

Chapter One
Designer Clothes

INTRODUCTION: Most women have at some time said (or thought), "I wish I could have just ONE custom made, one-of-a-kind DESIGNER outfit." We can — we can make it ourselves! We have the PATTERN from the greatest *designer* of all ages. If we follow this Pattern we can make a garment that will "clothe us in righteousness" and enable us to present it to the Designer, Himself, at the Last Day.

This garment will indeed be a "designer creation" if we use the pattern as directed. Our Designer created the Universe, our very own bodies, and He is the designer of our salvation. Our garment will be one-of-a-kind because we are individuals. Other women will use the same pattern, but their *material* will be different. Your material will be YOU — your talents, your opportunities and your time.

If we really desire this individually styled garment during our life time, we must begin *today*. Time is running out — we must recognize the urgency. This is not only the garment we will enjoy wearing every day for the remainder of our lives, it is the garment that the world will see.

Let's observe some well known facts about sewing and apply them to Christian living:

1. Decide that we WANT a new look
2. Select a pattern
3. Pick out material and notions
4. Count the cost
5. Take to check-out counter

Hurry home and start on that garment designed to give us a new look!

I. DECIDE WE WANT A NEW LOOK: We decide that we are tired of our rags, our lives of frustrations and indecisions. We determine in our hearts to become a "new creation" in Christ.

> Wherefore if any man is in Christ he is a new creature:
> the old things are passed away; behold they are become
> new (2 Corinthians 5:17).

This is a big decision, and with any decision there must be a commitment. We are contemplating a new life style, traveling on a different road, taking a journey that often is beset with trials, sacrifices and the temptation to turn back. But are we committed?

To make any journey, there must be the first step. On this journey the first step is to secure a book of instructions. The Holy Spirit emphasizes this — once in the Law of Moses (Deuteronomy 4:2), once by a Proverb writer (Proverbs 30:6), and again in Revelation 22:18, the present dispensation. This last admonition is in the *last* book of the Bible, the *last* chapter and almost His *last* words. The Holy Spirit wants us to remember!

II. SELECT A PATTERN: Find the best pattern available. The best often costs more because it is of better quality and will produce a more beautiful garment. IT IS WORTH THE PRICE.

The best pattern on the market is "Great Designer Pattern, UR #1" by Jesus Christ of Nazareth. Accept no substitute. Christ not only designed the pattern, He *is* the PATTERN. The apostle Peter spoke of this Pattern:

> Christ suffered for you, leaving you a pattern
> that ye should follow in his steps (1 Peter 2:21).

This "Designer Pattern" is none other than the Son of God, the Lion of the Tribe of Judah, the Root and the Offspring of David, the Rose of Sharon, the Lily of the Valley, the Bright and Morning Star, the Lamb Slain, but now STANDING — standing at the right hand of God. What a gorgeous pattern!

III. PICK OUT MATERIAL AND NOTIONS: What does the pattern call for? Read Galatians 5:22,23: *Love, Joy, Patience, Self-control* and other noble characteristics for a Christian's garment.

1. LOVE: Did you notice that the very first one is love? The Holy Spirit places love at the top of His list. Jesus also gives love top billing in all His teachings.

When asked "What is the greatest commandment?", Jesus answered: "Love the Lord thy God . . ." and then He added, "Love thy neighbor as thy self." Jesus knew mankind would have no trouble keeping all other commandments if he would master these two. For instance:

> Would a man kill another man if he loved him?
>
> Would one steal from his neighbor if he loved him?
>
> Love seems to be the vital ingredient of Christian living.

First Corinthians thirteen is called the LOVE CHAPTER of the Bible. Of all the things listed by Paul, he stresses that the greatest is love. Love does not "keep books" on people who treat others unkindly, or on those who would do them evil.

All needed material and notions (fruit of the Spirit listed in Galatians 5) are wrapped *in* and tied *with* LOVE. Read, then reread, the last part of verse 23. "Against these things there is no law." Imagine a policeman knocking on our door and forbidding us to be gentle, to use patience or to have joy and peace. Imagine him saying, "In the name of the law, I forbid you to love your neighbor." A good thing to put on our prayer list would be to thank Our Heavenly Father that there is no law against these things. In 1 Timothy 2:1,2 Paul exhorts us to do that very thing:

> I exhort therefore . . . that supplications, prayers, inter-
> cessions, thanksgivings, be made for . . . all that are in
> high places; that we may lead a tranquil and quiet life
> in all godliness and gravity.

Love is the key that unlocks the heart. It is the focus of our daily living for Christ. We cannot pray with an unforgiving attitude or with hatred in our heart.

We love only because Christ loved us. We can love even our enemies because Christ loved us. We love the unlovable because He loved us. We love because He loved. A lawyer can be a good lawyer without loving his client; a doctor can be a good doctor without loving his patient; but a Christian cannot be a good Christian without loving others.

A famous theologian was asked, "In all of your studies and your teachings what is the most profound thought that you have ever had?" The renowned theologian replied: "Jesus loves me. *This* I know, because the Bible tells me so."

Another example of simple, trusting faith is found in a story of a disabled person. A Christian woman who was confined to a wheel chair, wholly dependent on others for her every need, was asked how she spent her days. The answer: "I talk to God through prayer for a few hours each day, then He talks to me through His word for a few hours, then I just sit here and let Him love me." We have heard the saying "Love makes the world go 'round . . ." It certainly does for that Christian lady!

2. JOY: Joy is more than wearing a smile, although a smile communicates in any language. Joy is that deep feeling of serenity that comes from living with a good conscience, assured that we have ONE who understands when we falter and will help us to overcome. Joy gives that inward *peace* which is another material for our garment mentioned in Galatians 5.

When in a Roman prison, the Apostle Paul wrote to Christians in the city of Philippi: "Rejoice . . . again I say rejoice." QUESTION: How could one have joy and peace without love?

3. PATIENCE & SELF-CONTROL: To be patient means more than enduring. We often endure with the wrong attitude. The word *patient* is translated "long-suffering" in some versions of the Bible. Too many of us prefer that rendition solely because exercising patience causes us to suffer — and we suffer long! The biblical meaning is steadfastness. To be steadfast means to endure hardships, trials and temptations without allowing our faith to waver. This furnishes one other piece of material — SELF-CONTROL.

We are all experts at controlling others, yet how do we rate in controlling our own thoughts, words and actions? Much of self-control comes with maturity, but always it must be an acquired trait of our personality. "So teach us to number our days, that we may get a heart of wisdom" (Psalm 90:12). Again we ask, "How can one be patient and have self-control without love?"

Every requirement in this Pattern has a purpose. Our garment will be incomplete, and certainly not perfect, if even one material is omitted or if something extra is added. We want to make it like the Designer planned, don't we? When God made us He made us perfect — He "saw that it was good."

IV. COUNT THE COST: What is the price tag for this beautiful Designer Garment? Can we afford it? What are we willing to pay? Jesus asks a question in Luke 14:28:

> What man among you desiring to build a tower, does
> not first sit down and count the cost?

One way to determine whether or not we are willing to pay the price for this garment is to examine our priorities. What is *most important to our lives*? Less important? *NOT* important? Are we willing to pay the price? Can we afford NOT to? Can we possibly find the time to work on this garment? No, we cannot *find* time — we must *take* time!

The Apostle Paul, who suffered beatings, imprisonment, hunger and persecutions, and finally unjustly put to death could say:

> I reckon that the sufferings of this present time are not
> worthy to be compared with the glory which shall be
> revealed to us (Romans 8:18).

Paul paid a big price for the material in his garment, worked long hours for many years. He followed THE PATTERN! By all means read 2 Timothy 4:7 and 8. For good measure (we all want good measure when buying material) memorize Philippians 4:13: "I can do all things in him who strengtheneth me."

V. TAKE TO CHECK-OUT COUNTER: We take the pattern, material and the notions to the check-out counter. The clerk rings up the price of the material and notions, but surprises us by saying: "The Pattern is FREE." The clerk adds: "It is a gift from the Designer. His only requirement is that you follow His instructions."

The Designer Pattern, UR #1 is free! Jesus bought it with His blood and has given it to us. Paul says in 1 Corinthians 6:19, "Ye are not your own, for you were bought with a price."

Man is saved by the wonderful grace of God. This "grace of God" is Jesus who came to earth, made in the likeness of men, and brought salvation to all who will accept it.

The following poem illustrates the grace and love of God:

Heaven's Grocery Store

I was walking down life's highway a long time ago.
One day I saw a sign that read Heaven's Grocery Store.
As I got a little closer, the door came open wide
And when I came to myself, I was standing inside.

I saw a host of Angels; they were standing everywhere!
One handed me a basket and said, "My child shop with care."
Everything a Christian needed was in that grocery store,
And all you couldn't carry, you could come back for more.

First, I got some Patience; Peace was in the same row.
Farther down was Understanding — needed everywhere you go.
I got a box or two of Wisdom, a bag or two of Faith; and I
Couldn't miss the Holy Spirit for He was all over the place!

I stopped to get some Strength and Courage
To help me run this race.
By then my basket was getting full,
But I remembered that I needed some Grace.

As I went up the aisle I saw Prayer and I had to put that in
For I knew when I stepped outside I would run right into sin.
Love and Joy were plentiful; they were on the TOP shelf.
Songs and Praises were hanging near so I just helped myself.

I didn't forget Salvation — for Salvation, that was free.
So I tried to get enough of that to save both you and me.
Then I started up to the counter to pay my grocery bill,
For I thought I had everything to do my Master's will.

I said to the Angel at the check-out stand, "How much do I owe?"
He just smiled and said, "Take them everywhere you go."
I smiled right back and said, "Now really, how much do I owe?"
With a tender look He said, "My child, Jesus paid your bill
A long time ago."

—Author Unknown

This beautiful poem clearly points out that all of the necessary qualities of Christian living have been supplied by the grace of God through His Son Jesus.

One phrase in the poem — "I got a bag or two of Faith" — can serve as our motto as we labor on the project that we are committed to finish. We must have faith that we can "do all things through Christ" and have confidence in our ability to "Be all we can be."

The second part of this lesson will be CUTTING AND SEWING, but before we begin that study let's read the "Faith chapter" of the Bible — Hebrews eleven.

Faithfully Yours,
Farris

THINK ON THESE THINGS

1. If all use the same pattern, how can *our* garment be different?

2. What chapter is called the "Love Chapter" of the Bible?

3. CHALLENGE: Commit that chapter to memory.

4. With a decision comes ________________________ .

5. What warning do you find in the following scriptures?

    (a) Deuteronomy 4:2________________________

    (b) Proverbs 30:6________________________

    (c) Revelation 22:18________________________

6. What is the subject of Hebrews, chapter eleven?

Chapter Two

Designer Clothes, Part 2

INTRODUCTION: We are eager to begin on our new garment, but wait! There are some preliminary preparations before we begin to cut and sew. Let's check the pattern to see which step needs to be taken first. It should be no surprise to find that the *first* step is to read the instructions. All too often we simply go by the old adage: *When all else fails, read the instructions.*

I. READ INSTRUCTIONS: When we want to know what the Designer had in mind we must read his plans. This certainly applies to the pattern for our daily lives as we live in accordance with the instructions of **The Great Designer. Jesus has been tried and tested — we can know that His instructions are reliable. In HIS BOOK we read:**

> **Study to show thyself approved unto God; a workman**
> **that needs not be ashamed, rightly dividing the word of**
> **truth (2 Timothy 2:15).**

When Jehovah gave Moses instructions to build the Tabernacle, and how to make the elaborate curtains and furnishings, He said: "Now see that thou make them *according to the pattern* **that I have shown you" (Emphasis mine). In Lesson 1 the clerk at the checkout counter said: "The Pattern is free. It is a gift from the Designer. His only requirement is that we follow His instructions."**

The only liberty we have is to choose our own material (our own talents, personality, etc.). Our talents, personalities, backgrounds, environments and opportunities are different from all others and each garment will reflect this. All use the same Pattern but each garment will be One-of-a-Kind.

Studying God's Instructions in His word is necessary not only to follow the pattern but for our own salvation. At the same time this study equips us to teach others. We become a pattern for those around

us. For example, The Bible is full of admonitions to teach our children, and warns of the consequences if we do not. Jehovah speaks through His prophet Hosea (3:6):

> My people are destroyed for lack of knowledge; because thou has rejected knowledge I will also reject thee . . . and seeing thou has forgotten the law of thy God, I also will forget your children.

Through another prophet The Holy Spirit records:

> Behold the day will come saith the Lord Jehovah that I will send a famine in the land . . . not a famine of bread, nor a thirst for water, but of hearing the words of Jehovah (Amos 8:11).

The construction of our new garment involves keeping our priorities straight. Certainly one of these priorities should be to acquire a knowledge of God's word.

The Recruiting Department of the United States Army has a slogan: "Be All You Can Be." We want to "be all *we* can be" in making our garment. We do not want to be ashamed to present it to the Lord when He comes. The beloved John speaks to us: "And now, my little children abide in him . . . that you may not be ashamed before him at his coming" (I John 2:28).

Have faith in the Designer and do your best. That is all that the Lord requires of His children.

II. TAKING MEASUREMENTS: What a tape measure can reveal! We must face reality, especially in making our *old* lives into *new*. Let's face it — if our measurements are not what they should be, then we must change them accordingly. The Inspired Instructions certainly can help.

> Search me, O God, and know my heart: try me and know my thoughts; and see if there be any wicked way in me, and lead me in the way everlasting. (Psalm 139:23,24).

> Try your own selves, whether ye are in the faith. (2
> Corinthians 13:5)

The Holy Spirit is advising us to take our measurements (evaluate ourselves), and His advice is never wrong. Sometimes instructions are hard to understand and harder still to follow, so we must read them time and again.

1. HOW WIDE IS OUR UNDERSTANDING? How do we feel about a person of a different culture, someone with a different background socially or economically? Our "measurements" in this area can't be taken with an ordinary tape measure — we need a ruler made of gold. The GOLDEN RULE will solve many problems, and will help us to make changes in our lives.

2. HOW LONG IS OUR PATIENCE? The word *patience* has a dual meaning. It is defined "to endure", but it also means "to be steadfast"; "holding on when the going gets rough." Enduring — not temporarily nor with a rebellious attitude, but keeping calm amid the storms and seeing them through.

Patience is especially hard when we try to teach others. We wonder: Why in the world can't they understand? Often we forget that much learning is done by repetition. Remember how long it took to learn the multiplication tables? Upon close examination of our measurements (evaluation) in the area of patience we may be surprised!

3. HOW DEEP IS OUR LOVE? When we memorize and *practice* I Corinthians 13 we will discover our measure of love. (For a fuller discussion on love, see Lesson I, under topic LOVE).

III. STRAIGHTEN MATERIAL AND PIN TO PATTERN: Before we cut into our beautiful material there is one more important step. We must straighten the material — a wrinkle can make a big difference. Jesus wants to present the church to the Father "without spot or wrinkle" (Ephesians 5:27).

Christians are the church and the garment they are wearing when Christ returns must be free of all wrinkles. Our lives, then, must be straightened out.

We live in a "pressure-cooker" world. The world with all its pressures pushes us into a mold and we often conform to that mold. The Apostle Paul says, "Be not conformed to the world: but be ye transformed" (Romans 12:2). Transformation implies *change*. How can we change? Paul gives us the answer: "By the renewing of your mind." A wonderful scripture to memorize (and practice) is:

> Set your mind on the things that are above, not on the
> things that are upon the earth. (Colossians 3:2).

The *things* mentioned by Paul could be social prestige, career, bigger and better houses, cars and boats, family pleasures, clothes, jewelry, etc. That old "thief of time", procrastination, also robs us of time we should use in service to God.

In Acts, chapter three, a beggar asked Peter and John for money. In verse six, Peter says: "Silver and gold have I none; but what I have, that give I thee." Are we guilty of reversing what Peter said? Do we say, "I have silver and gold, and I will give to thee, but don't ask me to give of my time or myself?" Writing a check is easier than visiting the sick, cooking a meal for the needy or having a home Bible study.

Another important step before cutting the material is to *pin the pattern to the material.* Secure the material to the pattern; make sure it does not slip. The material and pattern must bond. In like manner we must secure our salvation by bonding to Christ.

> Make your calling and election sure (2 Peter 1:10).

> Let no man deceive you with empty words. (Ephesians
> 5:6).

> We ought to give the more earnest heed to the things we
> have heard, lest we let them slip (Hebrews 2:1).

For example, in today's world of change there is a danger of taking one's salvation for granted, a danger of being deceived by empty words, or danger of allowing our morals to slip. Paul knew the danger of materials slipping when he admonished Timothy, "Hold fast the pattern of sound words" (2 Timothy 1:13).

We already have learned that Christ is the Pattern; we are the material. The two must bond. Materials can slip so easily! Make sure they are secured to the Pattern..

IV. CUTTING: At last we are going to cut into this expensive, beautiful material. One lady said that she never learned to sew because she was always afraid to cut into the material. She feared making a mistake. Sometimes we too are afraid of making mistakes and often we do. However, mistakes can be corrected, and even teach a valuable lesson. Then we can get on with our "sewing."

Spiritually, we all make mistakes. They too can be corrected and we can get on with our lives.

> If we confess our sins, he is faithful and righteous to forgive us our sins, and to cleanse us from all unrighteousness (1 John 1:9).

If the mistake in our sewing is large, then the repair work may show, but we still can use the material. We must not throw away our new garment! God does not throw us away as we seek to mend our mistakes. A forceful example of this is found in the story where the clay marred in the potter's hand. The potter reshaped and re-molded it! He did not discard it (Jeremiah 18:4).

So it is with our lives. We are the imperfect clay and often we mar in the hand of our Potter, who is Jehovah God. Our Potter does not discard us — He simply re-shapes us when we surrender our lives to Him. Regardless of what we have done, He wants to re-mold us into beautiful "creatures" worthy of His image.

> He knows our frame, He remembers we are dust (Psalm 103:14).

We find it advisable to examine our material before cutting. If there are flaws we must cut around them. The following are some flaws for which to watch:

    1. TEMPER: Temper and anger usually go together. What does our "How-To Hand-Book" say?

    A soft answer turneth away wrath (Proverbs 15:1).

    Be ye angry and sin not (Ephesians 4:26).

    Paul says in Ephesians 4:31, "Let all bitterness and wrath be put away from you." It is never pleasant to be around those who have grown bitter, who go around with a "sour" look on their face. There is nothing more beautiful or more delicious than a big, red apple. But — vinegar is made from apples that have grown sour!

    2. GOSSIP: Sometimes in an *unguarded* moment we become angry and let our temper get out of control, but with gossip it is different. Gossip is deliberate and often malicious. Gossip can be facts, but all too often facts which are enlarged and embellished.

    A cartoon in a prominent newspaper depicted two women talking over the back fence. One said, "Oh? Tell me more!" The other woman replied, "I can't tell you more, I have already told you more than I heard." We may consider this funny, but gossip is no laughing matter. In Leviticus, chapter 19, Jehovah lists some sins in which His people should not engage. For example, there is lying, stealing, committing incest . . . and, among these heinous sins is gossip. Read verse 16 of Leviticus 19:

    Thou shalt not go up and down as a talebearer among
    thy people.

V. NOTIONS: *Finally,* we have our garment cut out, but before we begin to sew let's check our notions. (Have you noticed that notions are almost as expensive as the material?)

    1. ELASTIC: If we have the virtue of elasticity in our lives, along with forbearance, we will not pre-judge others without knowing all the facts. When we learn the facts we will be gentle toward a weaker sister. Remember, "until we walk in her shoes . . ."

    We will never compromise truth but we will be more elastic, more giving, more loving in our dealings with others. However, when the elastic becomes too tight we need to reread the teachings of our PATTERN in Matthew 7:1-5.

2. ZIPPER: A useful notion is a zipper. Zippers are used to close openings in skirts, dresses and other garments. At some time we all need a LIP ZIPPER to close our lips. The wise man Solomon said in Ecclesiastes, chapter 3, "There is a time for every thing under heaven . . . a time to keep silence and a time to speak."

"Silence is golden", someone has said. This is true but there is a time when we must *not* be silent. Speaking out on moral issues, Christian doctrines, etc., is necessary, but there are times when we find it better to be silent and "zip our lips."

3. STIFFENING: A seamstress would call it "pellon." Spiritually speaking, we call it courage. We must have the courage of our convictions. Peter was upbraided by Paul for not having courage. Peter would eat with Gentiles when no Jews were present.

How do we conduct ourselves when there are no other Christians present to see our actions or hear our words? We must not confuse this with being stiff-necked and unbending. This is where a Christian must walk a fine line. Someone has said, "A Christian is a well balanced person and a well balanced person is a Christian."

4. BINDING: We sometimes think of binding as one of those little notions. Binding, however, plays an important part in the construction of a garment. It was important to Jehovah in His instructions to His people.

> My son, keep the commandment of thy father, and forsake not the law of thy mother: Bind them continually upon thy heart (Proverbs 6:20,21).

All of the notions given by the Designer are essential for making a fine and complete garment. There is one notion, however, that is *not* called for in this Pattern, and that is ruffling. Don't get ruffled! Keep smiling!

VI. At last our garment is ready to be pressed. A compelling scripture comes to mind:

> Forgetting the things that are behind, and stretching
> forward to the things which are before, I press on ...
> (Philippians 3:13,14).

Forgetting that we were at one time as filthy rags before the Lord, *we press on* and put on our new Designer Garment. How sad it is that many of us walk around with the weight of guilt. We can't bring ourselves to believe that God has forgiven us, so we worry about past sins. If we sincerely repented of those sins, then God has not only forgiven us, HE HAS FORGOTTEN THEM. Why can't we forgive self? We should remember our past sins only as a reminder to avoid repeating them.

> ... though your sins be as scarlet,
> they shall be as white as snow;
> though they be red like crimson,
> they shall be as wool. If ye be
> willing and obedient ... (Isaiah 1:18,19).

CONCLUSION

We have taken lots of time, energy and money to make this garment. But isn't it beautiful? When it turned out according to the Pattern we began to forget the problems of adjustments (such as the waist line), and alterations (sleeve length). Now we can laugh when we remember that we sewed the collar on the wrong side (that was when we failed to study the instructions). We can *now* say with Paul that the reward is so great that we will forget all the troubles and trials.

Now we adorn ourselves with our *new* garment which we intend to wear every day for the remainder of our lives. We will wear it to the office, to PTA meetings, to the grocery store, to the laundry room and to parties. We will wear it when we visit in hospitals, when we attend civic meetings, when we go to worship and as we do our housework. The most important place of all is in the home, where we can display our "new look" and our "new self" in the presence of our family. May we ever wear it with dignity, grace and humility, befitting the daughters of the King.

Won't it be wonderful when we walk down that Runway at the "Heavenly Fashion Show" each displaying our self-made garment, made with the help of our perfect PATTERN? Each has been made with individual talents, each of different materials, yet all made by this Great Designer Pattern.

Christ paid for this Pattern — and what a price! He has left us an example: "For I have given you an example, that ye also should do as I have done to you" (John 13:15).

The Judge of *this* "fashion show" will be righteous and impartial. As we stand before Him in all our different garments — Yellow, Black, White or Red — suddenly they are all the same color, all dazzling WHITE! The Judge will say, ". . . these are they that washed their robes and made then white in the blood of the Lamb" (Revelation 7:14). While we await this glorious moment, let us wear our garments well and remember to give God all the Glory.

Faithfully Yours,
Farris

THINK ON THESE THINGS

1. Memorize 2 Timothy 2:15.

2. Read Exodus 25:9 and 40.

3. How important is it to follow instructions?

4. The "Farewell of Joshua" (Joshua 23:14-16) is a classic. How does this relate to following instructions?

5. Did you ever say something you wished later that you had not said? What does James say about this? (James 3:7,8).

6. Are you carrying around a load of guilt?

   Let Jesus help you (Matthew 11:28).

7. Are you *enjoying* "sewing" on your garment day by day? Class repeat Philippians 4:4 (individually or in unison).

8. Consult your "book of instructions" every day.

9. Let the "Faith chapter" of The Bible be your support as you wear your *new* garment for the world to see.

Chapter Three

Roads to Happiness

"Stand in the ways and see, and ask for the old paths, where the good way is, and walk in it; then you will find rest for your souls" (Jeremiah 6:16).

> "Would you tell me, please, which way I ought to go from here?" Alice asks the Cheshire cat in Lewis Carroll's *Alice in Wonderland.*
>
> "That depends a good deal on where you want to get to," said the cat.
> "I don't much care where," said Alice.
> "Then it doesn't matter which way you go, " said the cat.
> ". . . as long as I get *somewhere,*" Alice added as an explanation.
> "Oh, you're sure to do that," said the cat, "if you only walk long enough."

Like Alice, we too, are uncertain about which roads to take in life. Bewildered and confused by many roads, all going in different directions, we stand at the crossroads of decision.

Sometimes we simply do not know the way to take. One thing sounds good, then again something else appeals to us, too. God, speaking through Jeremiah, told the people to "choose the old paths, where the good way is."

The ultimate goal for most people is to find that path and in so doing, discover happiness. We as Christians are already on that road! Along the way, we will be confused by twists, turns and rocky places which wound and hurt. Pot-holes are there for us to fall into; and thorns which tear and snatch at our faith. Valleys appear into which we must descend, but surprisingly enough, so also are the hills unto which we can lift up our eyes.

The Christian road to happiness is a mixture of sadness and delight, yet all along our pilgrim journey, we can be sure He walks with us, leading us through the valleys up to higher ground.

STEP BY STEP

He does not lead us year by year
Nor even day by day.
But step by step our path unfolds;
Our Lord directs our way.
Tomorrow's plans we do not know.
We only know this minute;
But we will say, "This is the way,
By faith now walk ye in it."

— Author Unknown

Jeremiah 10:23 tells us: "Oh Lord, I know the way of man is not in himself; It is not in man who walks to direct his own steps."

No, it is not in and through ourselves that we will find the road to happiness. God has sent His Son, Jesus Christ, who told us, "I am the way."

His way is THE WAY to happiness. We have stood at the crossroads long enough. Let us choose the path that leads into everlasting happiness and joy — *the way* God wants us to go.

Unlike Alice and the cat, we are not just going "somewhere." We are pilgrims in search of a city. The ultimate goal in life is not happiness . . . it is to obtain heaven.

As we travel to heaven, there are countless serendipities — surprises that delight and amaze us. There is only one road to happiness — God's Way. Here are suggestions that will keep us on the "glory" road and bring us happiness along the way:

1. BEGIN EVERY DAY WITH GOD

It is amazing how much happiness is generated throughout the day when we begin our day with thoughts of God. Our first waking thought should be of Him. "Good morning, Father, thank You for this brand new day!"

No matter how sad or troublesome the day before has been, or how many tears we have shed in the night, we can begin our new day with this joyful attitude:

Weeping may endure for a night,
But joy comes in the morning.
(Psalm 30:5)

You see, joy comes to the heart of the Christian because God has brought us through the night and has given us the gift of another new day. We have twenty four hours ahead in which to make things better. "This is the day which the Lord has made, we shall rejoice and be glad in it" (Psalm 118:24).

God, our Father, longs for us to seek His face; to stand in His presence before all others. We read in His Word that most of the prophets and most of the people who followed God were the kind of people who arose early in the morning to worship and bow to Him.

It is so comforting in the morning to know that God is *here*. It is consoling to be able to look up to Him, to be still and think about Him, to know that no matter how hard our tasks — no matter how many difficulties we are going to face — God will hear our weakest prayers.

If we are still long enough to let our requests be known to Him, we shall be better equipped to face our day. We will have more confidence, more assurance, when we begin our day in Bible study and prayer.

How essential then are these first crucial moments of our day. After talking with our Father, we will be able to go about our work with more purpose and will be able to do our work with much more efficiency.

> My voice You shall hear in the morning, O Lord;
> In the morning I will direct it to You.
> And I will look up (Psalm 5:3).

2. PRACTICE THE PRESENCE OF GOD ALL DAY LONG

"Draw near to God, and He will draw near to you" (James 4:8). Practicing the presence of God will make a fantastic difference in the way you and I conduct ourselves. We will not want to sin or disappoint the Lord.

We need to know He is right here with us, living inside us. We deprive ourselves of a blessing when we fail to practice the presence of God. God is not a God who is far away (Acts 17:27) — One to whom we cannot approach. He is "at hand" (Philippians 4:5). He is as near as our heartbeats.

It is true that God waits for us to "open the door" to His presence. Then He promises us, "I will come in to him and dine with him, and he with Me" (Revelation 3:20.) That's a pretty intimate relationship.

God is "our refuge and strength, a very present help in trouble" (Psalm 46:1). He stands waiting for us to find Him. He also tells us, "You will seek Me and find Me, when you search for Me with all your heart" (Jeremiah 29:13). All day we should be seeking for and searching for the Lord.

God is always with us, always inside, always waiting to help and always by our sides. Jesus told His disciples that their hearts were not to be troubled. He went on to say, "Peace I leave with you, My peace I give to you; not as the world gives do I give to you. Let not your heart be troubled, neither let it be afraid" (John 14:27).

How can we know the happiness which comes from the presence of the Lord daily? By practicing it! By continually keeping the Lord near. He is as near as we place Him!

> In Your presence is fullness of joy;
> At your right hand are pleasures forevermore.
> (Psalm 16:11)

3. DEVELOP A CHILD-LIKE TRUSTING FAITH IN GOD

A child-like trust in God will bring us happiness no matter the circumstances. We will possess a bubbling confidence, knowing our heavenly Father is taking good care of us day by day.

A child has no reservations about trusting his father, does he? He believes his dad can do anything — he does not hesitate to bring every problem or care to him. His daddy will know what to do; his daddy loves him and can solve everything. This is what we believe about our earthly fathers.

Even more than our earthly fathers, we have a firm confidence in our Heavenly Father. He always knows just what is best for us. We can rest our hopes in Him and He will provide all our needs.

> And my God shall supply all your need according to
> His riches in glory by Christ Jesus (Philippians 4:19).

Faith in a Great God

There was a woman who was well known about her own area for her simple faith and her great calmness in the midst of trials. Another woman living at a distance, hearing of her, said: "I must go and see that woman, and learn the secret of her strong and happy life."The seeker inquired, "Are you the woman with the great faith?"

"No," she replied, "I am not the woman with the great faith; but I am the woman with the little faith in the great God."

There's the secret: God is omnipotent; and when we trust in Him there is nothing He cannot do for us; He can work in us abundantly, even above all we dare to ask or think (Ephesians 3:20).

—Author Unknown

I am sure that if you have read any of my books, you know the little verse which has kept me strong throughout my years:

> Trust in the Lord with all your heart,
> And lean not on your own understanding;
> In all your ways acknowledge Him,
> And He shall direct your paths.
> (Proverbs 3:5,6)

Notice these happy promises found in Psalm 5:11 and 12:

> Let all those rejoice who put their trust in You;
> Let them shout for joy, because You defend them;
> Let those also who love Your name be joyful in You.
> For You, Lord, will bless the righteous;
> With favor You will surround him as with a shield.

Look at the lessons we learn from these verses:

We will have great reason for rejoicing as we put our trust in Him.
We will not only have joy, we will want to *shout* for joy.
We will be joyful because His love is in our hearts.
When we are righteous we will be blessed (made happy).
We will be surrounded with grace (favor) like a shield.

Hurts and Pain

Despite everything, we all experience trials. Everyone has experienced the heaviness which accompanies sorrow or loss at one time or another. We speak of having a "heavy heart" or a "heavy" responsibility. Heaviness implies going through something difficult. One of its definitions is "hard to lift or move because of its weight."

We all know how it feels. The weight of grief or pain seems insurmountable. We are burdened and cannot seem to put our burden down. The burden just stays and stays, and we don't believe it will ever "move" or "go away." There seems to be no relief or lift anywhere we turn. The situation seems unendurable; it weighs us down with sadness.

Yet, in God's Word we are told we can experience deep down joy and happiness even in the midst of trials:

> Wherein ye greatly rejoice, though not for a season, if need be, ye are in heaviness through manifold temptations (1 Peter 1:6). KJV

Beloved, do not think it strange concerning the fiery trial which is to try you, as though some strange thing happened to you; but rejoice to the extent that you partake of Christ's sufferings, that when His glory is revealed, you may also be glad with exceeding joy (1 Peter 4:12,13).

God Himself gives us a garment to cover us during the heavy winter seasons. This garment is called "the garment of praise." How thankful we are that God gives us the "garment of praise for the spirit of heaviness" (Isaiah 61:3). As we go through our "seasons of heaviness" we shall continually need the warmth and security of the garment of praise.

THE TEST

It's easy to smile when the sun shines
And all the world is delight,
When life holds a dream, and joys are supreme
With everything lovely and bright.

It's easy to always be happy
When life is a beautiful song,
With never a care, and skies always fair
And nothing it seems can go wrong.

It's easy with never a trouble
A rainbow so bright in your sky,
But life is the best, when you will meet the test
Despite every heartache and sigh.

The real test of courage undaunted
Is to walk through the storm clouds or rain,
To never give in, but to still try again
And be happy despite hurts and pain.

—Garnett Ann Schultz

One of the most remarkable statements in the Bible is found in Romans 8:31:

What then shall we say to all these things? If God is for us, who can be against us?

It takes a lot of trust and faith to believe that statement. But as someone has well said, "If God is for us, who can be against us?"

4. THINK HAPPY, POSITIVE THOUGHTS ALL DAY

We are what we think about all day. "For as he thinks in his heart so is he" (Proverbs 23:7). Our thoughts will make us or break us. We choose the attitudes of our heart — the attitude we take toward any given situation is determined by our thoughts. As we consistently think good, wholesome thoughts, we will manifest good, wholesome deeds.

In the process of turning our thoughts toward God, we'll soon find God is transforming us by the renewing of our minds (Romans 12:2).

Colossians 3:2 tells us: "Set your mind on things above, not on things on the earth." This is not something which happens automatically — thinking is hard work. To think godly thoughts, we've got to rid ourselves of old, negative thoughts. How can we do this? By replacing them little by little with new, positive, happy thoughts.

Remember 2 Corinthians 10:5? We are to "demolish arguments and every pretension that sets itself up against the knowledge of God, and we take captive every thought to make it obedient to Christ." (NIV)

The thought life of a Christian is his most powerful possession. We have the power to be amazingly happy, cheerful and optimistic because Christ lives in our minds. Actively practicing "having the mind (attitude) of Christ" within, brings inexplicable joy.

Jesus stated positively:

> Therefore you now have sorrow; but I will see you again and your heart will rejoice, and your joy no one will take from you (John 16:22).

Will you choose to be happy today no matter what the circumstances, or will you allow circumstances, people or things to get the best of you? "Choose for yourselves this day whom you will serve:" (Joshua 24:15).

5. CULTIVATE A SUNNY, CHEERFUL SPIRIT

So often our dispositions are determined by circumstances, people and even the weather. A child of God knows that joy and peace of mind are not determined by any of these things. Should we allow people, things and circumstances to rule our lives, none of us would ever be happy.

The world is crowded, even over-populated, with people who will discourage us, things that upset us, and situations which dismay us. If we are unhappy with the place where we are, the people we are with, and things that are happening to us, we can make the situation better by manifesting Christian cheerfulness.

Once we learn the joyful and precious fact that we determine our own happiness and cheer, we can then proceed to "get on" with our lives in uplifting, beautiful ways.

How is joy and cheer generated in a person's life? A cheerful, merry heart and disposition comes from "abiding in Him and He in you." It comes from *knowing the Lord!*

Psalm 37:4 tells us, "Delight yourself in the Lord, and He shall give you the desires of your heart."

Don't you love being around sunshiny people? Of course, we all do. Some of their joy seems to rub off on us. As a result, we feel better . . . more able to cope with things, more encouraged . . . happier inside.

Perhaps you, too, will want to "spread a little sunshine" on the next person you meet. Happiness multiplies and grows as we share it with others. Cheerfulness is a gift God gives us because He loves us so. Joy has its origin in Him. All resources of joy come from the Father above. His presence within causes us to overflow like a fountain.

> Let all those who seek You rejoice and be glad in You;
> Let such as love Your salvation say continually, "the
> Lord be magnified!" (Psalm 40:16).

With gladness of heart, rejoicing in His salvation, we pass on happiness and joy to others. David Dunn said in his little book *Try Giving Yourself Away:*

"Happiness is one of the greatest gifts within the power of any of us to bestow, particularly in these troubled days when the world is full of fear and suspicion, and men's minds and hearts are anxious."

TALK HAPPINESS

Talk happiness. The world is sad enough
Without your woe. No path is wholly rough;
Look for the places that are smooth and clear,
And speak of those, to rest the weary ear
Of earth, so hurt by one continuous strain
Of human discontent and grief and pain.

— Author Unknown

"Talk happiness. The world is sad enough." How true! Joe Barnett said, "Joy is that quality of glad-heartedness which is produced by being wrapped up in God." We all need to wrap ourselves daily in God. As the day goes on, we can slowly unwrap ourselves, bestowing God's grace and love on others.

6. BEGIN EARLY IN THE MORNING GIVING YOURSELVES AWAY

The most miserable people in the world are those who live only for themselves. The happiest people are those who forget themselves in service to others. Developing the servant's spirit is one of the happiest things we shall ever do for ourselves. God designed us to be serving people! In Ephesians 2:10, Paul made this statement:

For we are His workmanship (work of art), created in Christ Jesus for good works, which God prepared before hand that we should walk in them (Parenthesis — my thoughts).

In my devotional book *New Day Dawning* I wrote the following thoughts:

The farmer begins sowing his seed in the early hours of the morning, doesn't he? In the same way, we as *His* harvesters, need to begin our service for others at the beginning of the day. Opportunities for service occur at any time of the day, but I have noticed that those performed at the earliest possible moment bring the sweetest rewards.

We begin on our knees, asking God to show us opportunities to manifest kindness, love and comfort. God will provide the "happenstance" wherein we may serve.

The longer I live, the deeper I believe we as women are called to full time service for the Lord. I believe women are given a warmer nature, a more compassionate spirit, because we know the Lord Jesus Christ. He abides in us to spread warmth and love among all those who come into our area of service.

Everyday God calls us to service. May we follow the wonderful example of God's Son as he gave His life in service to others. May we never let one day slip away without sowing seeds of kindness.

Jesus, after washing His disciple's feet, told His band of men: "If you know these things, happy are you if you do them" (John 13:17).

Jesus stated this important truth in the context of knowing He would soon depart this earth. However long our lives, the true secret of happiness is found in serving others.

7. SHARE YOUR FAITH CONTINUALLY

If our faith is worth having it is worth sharing. If He means anything at all to us, we can't help talking about His goodness and merciful kindness.

We should be like the man whom Jesus advised:

> Go home to your friends, and tell them what great things the Lord has done for you and how He has had compassion on you (Mark 5:19).

Sowing tiny seeds in the ground and watching them sprout, bloom and blossom is a wondrous thing. Planting the heavenly seed of God's Word is even more wondrous. The Seed is God's Word and we are the sowers. The happiest experience of life is the saving of lost souls. I love this Psalm:

> They that sow in tears,
> Shall reap in joy,
> He that goes forth weeping
> Bearing precious seed
> Shall doubtless come again rejoicing
> Bearing his sheaves with him.
>   (Psalm 136:5,6)

Who hasn't experienced the joy which comes after we have taught and led someone to Christ? We miss such a blessing when we fail to share the gospel with our friends and loved ones. There is nothing more rewarding than seeing a lost soul brought to salvation — knowing he now has forgiveness of his sins. What is more:

> Let him know that he who turns a sinner from the error of his way will save a soul from death and cover a multitude of sins (James 5:20).

If we have failed to find true happiness and joy, we will certainly find it in "bearing precious seed" to the lost.

8. CULTIVATE A SPIRIT OF ADVENTURE AND WONDER

We discover renewed joy and meaning in our lives when we approach each new day with excitement and expectation. What new adventure does the Lord have in store today? We usually find that which we are looking for.

Adventuring will bring added zest and flavor to our lives. It will help us overcome boredom, tedium and forever moving in the same old ruts. It will give us a sense of expectancy as we wait to discover the remarkable things the Lord will bring about today.

Our God is a God of surprises!

He surprises us with extraordinary pleasures if we look for them. The secret is being tuned in to Him and the wonders of His ways.

Someone has written:

> While the "happyologists" are searching for scientific clues to human happiness, we need only turn to God's Word to find that the highest form of happiness comes from fellowship with Jesus Christ.
>
> > We mutter and sputter;
> > We fume and we spurt;
> > We mumble and grumble,
> > Our feelings get hurt;
> > We can't understand things,
> > Our vision grows dim,
> > When all that we need is
> > A moment with HIM.
> > — Author Unknown

Observant and aware of the unexpected tokens of His love, we will look for evidences of His presence among us.

My friend, Ruby Jones, who writes a column entitled "Odds 'n' Ends" for an Indiana paper caught my attention with these words:

> Did you ever happen to enter the freeway and suddenly a huge sign leaped into view: "Go back!" "You are going the wrong way!" it warns. If you didn't obey, you might be headed for a fatal accident. In the same way there are road signs for us, too, in the matter of making the right decision . . . of waiting patiently for the green go-ahead signal; of turning back when the sign reads "Dead End."
>
> Learn to read the signs aright by having the willingness to ASK for guidance, cultivate the willingness to WAIT, and the willingness to OBEY . . . and if you are hammering on a door that doesn't want to open, just make up your mind that quite possibly that door doesn't have your name on it, and so you should try another . . . and when you find the right one, you can march through triumphantly and be on your way.

Yes, we all misread the road signs sometimes and knock on the wrong doors, but if we pay attention God will teach us some remarkable truths along the way.

We don't need a lot of money in the bank to make us feel secure. Do we need prestige, power, fame or even approval to feel really loved?

All we really need is "God in us" which is the root meaning of the word *enthusiasm*. "All we need to make us really happy is something to be enthusiastic about" someone has said. The Father has told us, "I will never leave you, nor forsake you," and with such a promise we can walk down happiness road, enthusiastically and thankfully all the days of our lives.

Life is always an adventure, full and overflowing, when God is near. In His presence is "fullness of joy." The road to happiness leads HOME. You and I can choose to walk that road, for He walks beside us all the way.

You will show me the path of life: in your presence is fullness of joy; at your right hand there are pleasures for evermore (Psalm 16:11).

Faithfully Yours,
Judy

THINK ON THESE THINGS

1. God, through Jeremiah, "_____ _____ _____ _____, where the _____ _____ is."

2. What is the ultimate goal of most people?

3. The Christian road to happiness is a mixture of ___________ and _________.

4. What happens in the process of drawing nearer to God?

5. How can we know the happiness which comes from the presence of the Lord daily?

6. When is the best time of day to seek God? Why?

7. Where is "fullness of joy" found?

8. A _________ _____ ______ in God, will bring us happiness no matter the circumstances.

9. If God supplies all our needs (Philippians 4:19) how can we be unhappy?

10. Why are our thoughts important?

11. How are our attitudes determined?

12. Do we have a choice about our attitudes?

13. Who are the most miserable people in the world?

14. Life is an _______________ when God is _______.

Chapter Four

Thank You Lord for Trees

TREES: The American poet Joyce Kilmer (1886-1918) wrote:

I think that I shall never see
A poem as lovely as a tree . . .
Poems are made by fools like me,
But only God can make a tree.

The wonder of how a tree grows is surpassed only by its beauty!

A tree grows from the roots upward. The roots sustain it, sending growing power to each branch and every leaf. Leaves fall, branches die and are pruned from the tree, but as long as the roots are alive new branches will sprout. Leaves will also appear and the tree will bring forth fruit and once again reproduce itself.

Trees provide a welcome shade from the hot sun. From trees we get lumber to build our houses and wood to cook our food. In ancient times trees were the only source of fuel for cooking.

I am saddened to think that millions of trees are burned each year in forest fires, usually started by a careless match or by a camp fire that has not been entirely extinguished. Millions of trees are felled yearly to provide us with what we have come to think of as being necessary for our life-style. Paper and thousands of paper by-products are made from trees.

I cannot waste paper! I am *miserly* with paper. I see a beautiful tree giving its life for the paper that I am using at this moment. One of my dear friends supplies me with discarded business forms from her office that would otherwise be shredded. The rough draft of this lesson was made on some of those forms. I make my note pads from paper that normally would be thrown away. I take the unused portion at the bottom of business letters, cut them to uniform size and either staple them together or use a colorful tape at the top. (Most business firms use heavy, expensive stationery which makes pretty note pads.) These pads are useful for grocery lists, for writing notes to *myself* and for keeping near the phone for short messages. *Wasted paper means wasted trees.*

Books and many other materials used in class rooms have been made from trees, and in the Bible School class rooms most have been purchased with the Lord's money. Small children, and older students as well, should be taught to respect and care for these materials. It is appalling to see the disregard for tablets, note-books, "quarterlies" and the Bible. Yes, the Holy Bible! Bibles on the floor where they have been carelessly dropped, missing pages and covers torn off must all make the Holy Spirit sad. He directed "holy men of old" to write the Book, and the contents are spiritual. Children/students should be taught that this *is* a spiritual, Holy Book even though it is a book printed by men with ink and paper made by men. They should be taught that it is the *only* book that will take them from earth to heaven.

Today in Eastern Europe and other parts of the world, men and women are begging for a copy of the Holy Bible. Students of the World Bible School Correspondence Course plead with their instructors to send them a Bible! In some countries a Bible costs the equivalent of a month's wages, while in our country we can buy a copy for less than the price of a "burger and fries." Its enemies have tried to destroy it, but valiant men have given their lives to protect it. God's Providence has preserved it. Heaven and earth will pass away, but God's Word will abide forever. It will judge us at the Last Day. If you own a copy of the Holy Bible you have a copy of something that will go into eternity! Treasure it, handle it carefully, love it and obey it.

We must not forget that the pages in our Bible are made from trees. I love trees and each time I see one I want to shout: *thank you, Lord, for trees.*

EDEN'S TREES:

The trees in the Garden of Eden must have been very beautiful; made full grown, with blossoms and fruits to enhance them.

> And out of the ground made Jehovah God to grow every tree that is pleasant to the sight, and good for food; the tree of life also in the midst of the garden, and the tree of the knowledge of good and evil. (Genesis 2:9).

It took the mighty power of Satan (never underestimate his power) to cause mankind to disobey God's law and desecrate the mystical tree of "knowledge of good and evil." Jehovah God commanded the man to *not* eat of that tree — "for in the day that thou eatest thereof thou shalt surely die" (Genesis 2:17). But Adam and Eve *did* eat of that forbidden tree and from that time forward man is dying a spiritual death, unless he avails himself of a Redeemer.

Many lessons have been taught about Mother Eve enticing her husband to sin. With the reader's indulgence I would like to point out what I consider to be the greatest lesson of all for "daughters of Eve" — the influence of a woman! A woman's influence, whether it be for good or evil, is powerful. Her influence in the home as she lives within those four walls with her husband and children can make a difference in their destiny.

Man fell, and a price must be paid for his sins. The first hint of a Redeemer is recorded in Genesis 3:15:

> I will put enmity between thee and the woman, and
> between thy seed and her seed; he shall bruise thy head,
> and thou shalt bruise his heel.

Four thousand (4,000) years passed, "but when the fulness of the time came, God sent forth his Son, born of a woman . . ." (Galatians 4:4). Four thousand years seems to us to be a very long time, but "The Lord is not slack concerning his promise, as some count slackness . . . " (2 Peter 3:9). NOTE the place of women in God's Great Eternal Purpose and Plan.

THE GOPHER TREE:

Many trees reproduced themselves in the vast period of time since Adam and Eve and the time of Noah. In that *sixteen hundred years* the people grew unbelievably wicked. The thoughts and imaginations of their hearts were evil continually in God's sight. God decided to destroy every living thing — even man who was made in His image. What a sad day!

Then the Lord remembered a righteous man named Noah, with whom He renewed His promise to send a Redeemer. He told Noah that He would bring a flood upon the earth and destroy every living thing and every living creature. God commanded Noah: "Make thee an ark of gopher wood" (Genesis 6:14). After giving Noah specific instructions as to how he should build the ark, the Lord said to Noah: "But I will establish my covenant with thee; and thou shalt come into the ark, thou, and thy sons, and thy wife, and they sons' wives with thee" (Genesis 6:18). God's promise to save Noah, Mrs. Noah, their sons and their sons' wives was contingent upon Noah's obedience.

Jehovah commanded Noah to build the Ark of *gopher* wood. No other wood would do. When God specifies something, that rules out all else. Can you visualize Noah, Shem, Ham and Japheth felling enough gopher trees to build an Ark large enough to hold all the specified things, in addition to the eight people in the Noah family? I can! God commanded and Noah obeyed. God's law to man never changes. From the beginning of time it has always been the same: Believe Him, obey Him and He will bless you. Noah believed and obeyed. "By faith Noah . . . prepared an ark . . ." (Hebrews 11:7).

The rains came! The flood came! The Ark, filled with its precious cargo floated for over a year, not because gopher wood had some mystical power within itself, but because God had commanded Noah to build it out of gopher wood — and Noah built it out of gopher wood!

Eventually, the mighty Ark made from gopher trees came to rest upon Mount Ararat. The waters subsided and the eight souls within the Ark were saved according to God's promise. *God keeps his word.* Upon disembarking (in a spirit of reverence and thanksgiving) Noah offered a sacrifice to Jehovah which was accepted by Him. In return, Jehovah God made a covenant (promise) that He never again would destroy the earth with a flood. The covenant also was made to the animals and every living creature. (Dr. Doolittle was not the first to "talk to the animals," was he?) Jehovah then set the beautiful rainbow in the clouds as a reminder that the waters never again would destroy the earth and its inhabitants. This *reminder* was made not only for man, but to HIMSELF as well. He said, "When the bow is seen in the cloud, *I* will remember my covenant." *God keeps his word.*

SPECIAL NOTES ABOUT THE "FLOOD":

A study of the word "flood" is very interesting. In the original text it is used to describe a phenomenon and is never used again in the original except to refer to this awesome event. The word "flood" means to *mix, mingle, confound, confuse, agitate, stir up.* A flood such as this could change the topography, accounting for skeletons of large mammals found out of their natural habitat — having been carried about by the mixing and mingling of the whole universe. Sandy deserts were once beds of great waters. The plains of Russia are below sea level and only the ring of mountains which encircle them keeps them from again becoming a sea.

> . . . all the fountains of the great deep [were] broken up,
> and the windows of heaven were opened (Genesis 7:11).

The earth was again a chaotic, turbulent mass. Dry land which had appeared on the third day of Creation was "overwhelmed" by this great cataclysm, upsetting earth's surface. Valleys were formed, mountains torn asunder and every tree covered with water — from the beautiful Cedars of Lebanon, the gnarled Olive trees of Galilee, the Giant Redwoods to the smallest sprout in the forest. Only Jehovah could withdraw His Spirit from His natural elements to cause such a catastrophe, and only He could stop it. "Jehovah sat as king at the flood" (Psalm 29:10). God had said, "I will bring a flood." Only He can change His immutable law. Satan's power is *limited*. JEHOVAH SAT AS KING AT THE FLOOD.

We use the word "flood" to describe a river overflowing its banks, or street flooding that causes traffic to stall, but we have never seen a flood like the flood of Noah's time. Nor will we ever. All of earth's small streams and mighty rivers flow into the sea, but the seas never overflow. Nor will they ever. And we know why, don't we? The incomparable thirty-eighth chapter of Job tells us *why;*

> . . . Where was thou when I laid the foundations of the
> earth? . . . shut up the sea with doors . . . and marked out
> for it my bound, and set bars and doors, and said,
> Hitherto shalt thou come, but no further; and here shall
> thy proud waves be stayed?

And all because Jehovah sat as King (ruler) at the flood. He commanded, Noah believed and obeyed Him!

Let us not forget the heroic gopher trees that withstood it all. God could have kept an *iron* ship afloat, or He could have specified any other wood, but He said GOPHER and Gopher it must be. Of all the trees that

He made "in the beginning" the GOPHER TREE was chosen to keep alive God's Promise of a Redeemer (Genesis 6:18). What an honor for Gopher Trees!

A PROMISE MADE UNDER AN OAK TREE:

Over four hundred years have passed since God saved eight souls from the great flood. Four centuries have passed since He put His beautiful rainbow in the sky as a token to man that never again would there be such a flood. Oh, there was to be thunder, lightning and big rains (according to His natural laws) in the coming centuries, but never rains of this magnitude. Our streets will continue to be covered at times with heavy rains; small streams will continue to get out of their banks and newsmen will write about a flood . . . a flood to us, but not in the same sense that "flood" is used in Genesis. It will never rain to the extent that all the Universe will be covered. God said so, and GOD KEEPS HIS WORD.

Numberless trees sprouted, grew, shed their fruits for reproduction and died during those four centuries since Noah's time. Many changes took place. People were no longer of one race and one language. Men scattered to many parts of the earth and invented to themselves foreign gods — some worshiping TREES! God never intended for man to worship "the creature rather than the Creator" (Romans 1:25).

But there is always a "righteous remnant" who clings to the only true God. Of this righteous few we find Abraham and Sarah who pitched their tent in the shade of a magnificent oak tree in the village of Mamre. One day as Abraham was resting under this giant OAK he looked and saw three men approaching. He provided food for them. Genesis 18:8 says, "he stood by them under the tree" while they ate.

It was under the canopy of this *oak tree* that Jehovah promised Abraham and Sarah that they would have a son at the same time next year. This would be the son through whom the promised Redeemer would come. The Redeemer was prophesied in Genesis 3:15, over two thousand years ago! The Redeemer would save man from the spiritual death brought upon him through the fall of Adam (1 Corinthians 15:22).

This aged couple, far beyond child bearing years, believed Jehovah and had faith that He was able to carry out His Promise. Again we see the principle in operation: "Believe Him, obey Him and He will bless you." At the promised time Sarah bore a son — the first recorded "miracle child" — although at first she had no precedent for this conception and birth, yet she counted God able to carry out His promise (Hebrews 11:11). God continued to work His Plan of Redemption through a woman! Sarah is in the HALL OF FAITH (Hebrews 11) because she counted God faithful to KEEP HIS WORD.

Sarah and Abraham named their son Isaac. Was ever a son more loved? Did Isaac run and play under this Oak of Oaks? Then tragedy struck! Jehovah commanded Abraham to give this beloved son as a burnt offering to Him. The Holy Spirit does not tell us whether or not Sarah knew of this command and I am *glad* that He didn't. The Holy Spirit does tell us that Abraham counted God able to raise his son from death, although again we know of no precedent of a resurrection (Hebrews 11:17-19).

Abraham's faith was surely put to the test! The wood was on the altar. The species of tree from which this wood was taken is unknown to us, but whatever tree gave its life for this sacrifice must have bowed its branches in sorrow.

God commanded and Abraham believed and obeyed, but where is the blessing promised by God when these conditions are met?

Before the wood from this unknown tree was set afire, Abraham looked and

> . . . behold, behind him a ram caught in the thicket by
> his horns: and Abraham went and took the ram, and
> offered him for a burnt offering in the stead of his son
> (Genesis 22:13).

There is the blessing — *the Son of Promise* is saved! *God keeps His word.*

The promise made under that historic oak tree was the beginning of the Hebrew race. This chosen race was selected by God to be the medium by which He would reveal Himself to mankind. In founding the Hebrew nation, God's *immediate* object in His Great Eternal Plan was to establish (in a world of idolatry) the idea of ONE God. His ultimate aim in setting aside a particular people was to bring Christ into the world through a pure blood line. All this began under a TREE.

The Promise made under that beloved oak was also the beginning of the CHRISTIAN'S FAMILY TREE. Christians are the "children of promise" and are the true sons of Abraham through faith (Galatians 3:26-29). In Christ there is no Jew, no Gentile, no bond or free, but all are *one* in Christ Jesus, and are "Abraham's seed, heirs according to promise" (Galatians 3:29). The promise spoken of here is the promise that was made under an *Oak Tree* at Mamre centuries ago.

What about the Christian's Family Tree? Who is on this Family Tree? ANSWER: Every Christian who has lived since Pentecost A. D. 33. They have been placed alongside all those who lived faithfully in every age and every dispensation. There is still room for all those who will live "godly in Christ Jesus" until the end of time. It is somewhat like a relay race. Those who have gone before us have handed the torch to us. We must take it and run. We must not drop it! We must carry on this *spiritual* Family Tree.

Jehovah promised Abraham that through him and his seed "all the nations of the earth would be blessed" (Genesis 12:3). If Christians are the true seed of Abraham, if all nations are to be blessed through *his seed*, then Christians must "bless" them by taking the gospel *to* them and by living exemplary lives *before* them.

THANK YOU LORD FOR TREES. Thank you for the stately oak at Mamre and our *Promised Heritage through Abraham*. Thank you for our Christian Heritage through Christ and for our spiritual Family Tree!

ELIJAH'S JUNIPER TREE:

In the nine hundred and fifty years after the death of Abraham and Sarah, God's people multiplied until they could be numbered into the millions. Their beloved Isaac had two sons. It was to one of these sons, Jacob, that the Lord renewed His Promise of a Redeemer — a Messiah, the Savior of mankind. Jacob had twelve sons, later to father the Twelve Tribes of Israel. From the tribe of Judah (Abraham's great-grandson) would come that Redeemer, our Savior and Lord, Jesus the Christ. Many years later John would call Him "the Lion of the tribe of Judah" (Revelation 5:5).

The covenant that Jehovah made with the descendants of Abraham and Sarah was renewed *again* by the giving of a set of laws through His servant Moses. These laws include the Ten Commandments upon which moral laws of every known religion are based. Countries that do not believe in the *one* God, or in Jesus as His Son, still base their laws and code of ethics upon the Ten Commandments.

Centuries passed and the people demanded and got a king. One of their kings, King Ahab, was very wicked but his wife, Jezebel, was even more ungodly. After Jehovah's prophet Elijah proved the four hundred and fifty prophets of Jezebel to be false (in an exciting contest) Queen Jezebel sent word to him that she would have him killed before that time the next day. Space does not permit relating all the events in the life of Elijah but the record is found in 1 Kings 17 through 2 Kings 2.

Elijah fled from the wrath of Jezebel. He went into the wilderness and being tired, hungry, depressed and fearful he sat down under a *JUNIPER TREE* and asked Jehovah to take away his life. (Jezebel would have done that for him! After all, that is the reason he fled from her).

Elijah was desperate but he "laid himself down and slept." While asleep, an angel of Jehovah touched him and said, "Arise and eat." Elijah looked and there was a cake "baked" on hot stones and a cruse of water. Elijah ate and drank and "laid himself down again."

> The angel of Jehovah came again the second time and
> touched him and said Arise and eat because the journey
> is too great for thee (1 Kings 19:7).

Elijah arose, ate and drank and "went in the strength of that food forty days and forty nights unto Horeb, the mount of God: where he took shelter in a cave."

The Bible says, *"and behold, Jehovah passed by"* (emphasis mine). Then came a great wind, an earthquake and a fire, but Jehovah was not in any of them. In a *still, small voice* the Lord asked, "What are you doing here, Elijah?" Elijah explained to the Lord how Israel had forsaken His laws, had torn down His altars and slain His prophets. He added, "I only am left and they seek to kill me." Jehovah *listened* to His servant Elijah and assured him that things were not as bad as he thought them to be. Then the Lord did a surprising thing — He commanded Elijah to return to Damascus *where he had left his problems.*

All Christian women have at some time been frustrated, lonely, tired, afraid and discouraged. Often we feel we are all alone in our troubles and that no one cares. The Lord cares but we, like Elijah, must first face up to our problems, return to them and allow Christ to help us.

Elijah experienced these feelings to the extent that he *thought* he wanted to die, but he really didn't. To escape death is the reason he was under the Juniper Tree! He was weary and did not recognize the magnitude of what was happening — an angel caring for him. When his physical needs were attended to Elijah "laid himself back down." The angel touched him again and said, "Arise."

How many times have we missed seeing a cake baked by an "angel" because we were asleep? How many times have we accepted God's grace and then "laid ourselves back down again?" How many times has the Lord through one of His angels nudged us the second time to get up and try again? We, like Elijah, must *arise* and with the help of the Lord get on with His work. Are we listening to the still small voice, or are we waiting for a great wind, an earthquake or fire? Jehovah *listened* to His servant Elijah. He will listen to us . . . "let your requests be made known unto God" (Philippians 4:6).

Every Christian has her Juniper Tree. Do we use our tree to sit under and complain about our problems, or do we use it for a quiet place to retreat and talk to the Lord? Do we "sit still" and know that He is God? Do we let His Holy Spirit feed us through His word — then *arise* and go in the strength of that food to do His work? I love my Juniper Tree!

A POSTSCRIPT TO THE LIFE OF ELIJAH:

The life of Elijah was exciting, daring and heroic. He was fed by ravens, hunted by his enemies, touched by an angel and finally taken up to heaven in a "flaming chariot" by a whirlwind. This man who sought refuge under a Juniper Tree and asked God to take his life didn't experience death after all!

The next and last time that we read of Elijah is almost one thousand years later when he is in a glorified state standing with Moses and Christ on the Mount of Transfiguration! They were talking about the death of Jesus which "he was about to accomplish at Jerusalem" (Luke 9:31).

Elijah reached the pinnacle and there he will dwell in that glorified state forever with the Lord. What a beautiful end to the life of the great prophet — *the man who took shelter under a juniper tree. THANK YOU LORD FOR TREES.*

THE TREE OF BETHLEHEM:

Nine hundred years passed between Elijah under his Juniper Tree and the MANGER IN BETHLEHEM.

> When the fullness of the time came, God sent forth his Son, born of a woman, born under the law, that he might redeem them that were under the law, that we might receive the adoption of sons (Galatians 4:4,5).

Mary "brought forth her firstborn son, and laid him in a manger." A manger made from an unnamed TREE. The manger held the Redeemer that had been promised four thousand years ago. *The* Redeemer, born of a woman. God still was using women in His Great Eternal Plan!

As a young man growing up in the household of Mary and Joseph, Jesus was "subject unto them." We can rightly infer that He worked alongside Joseph in the carpenter shop. Many TREES were used in that carpenter shop in Nazareth. I like to think of Joseph and Jesus (and His brothers) tenderly shaping wood from these trees into baby beds, tables, chairs, chests, wooden locks and their keys, decorative work for door posts upon which scripture was nailed, and possibly fishing boats. Carpenters also made coffins in which to bury the dead ... all of these things from TREES.

THE TREE THAT BECAME A CROSS:

Of all the trees made by Elohim "in the beginning" there is one that stands out as the *saddest* tree of all — the Tree of Calvary — the Tree that became a Cross.

That Cross, fashioned from an *unnamed* TREE, held the Promised Redeemer suspended between Heaven and earth. For some four thousand years the promise of a Redeemer had kept hope alive for God's people — hope that some day ONE would come and set them free. Now one had come and was nailed to a TREE. Jesus gave His life as a sacrifice in order to redeem mankind.

We are reminded of another TREE that provided wood for a sacrifice when Abraham offered his son — that Son of Promise.

Happily, a substitute was found for that sacrifice (a ram) and Abraham offered it "for a burnt offering in the stead of his son" (Genesis 22:13). That substitute was an *unwilling* substitute, no doubt! But on the Tree of Calvary there was a *willing* substitute for us. The Son of Promise, Son of God, Son of Mary, willingly died on a TREE "in our stead" that we might live eternally.

Upon Calvary's Tree Jesus nailed (figuratively) the Law of Moses, because He was the fulfillment of that beautiful old law. He, Himself, said: "Think not that I came to destroy the law or the prophets; I came not to destroy, but to fulfill" (Matthew 5:17).

Jesus lived under the Law of Moses while in the flesh and that makes the Old Covenant more beautiful and precious to Christians. After all the Old Law is the "school master" that brought us to Christ, that we might be justified *by faith* (Galatians 3:24) and become the true sons of Abraham under a better covenant.

Calvary's Tree was the tree from which the Son of Mary and the Son of God cried, "Father, forgive them." Jesus died on that tree to save man, not to condemn him. He wants all men everywhere to come to a knowledge of truth and be saved.

That sad *TREE OF CALVARY* brought death and despair, yet it was an instrument of life and hope. Three days after that TREE held the crucified Jesus of Nazareth, He came forth from the grave and brought life and immortality to all who will believe and obey Him. God's basic law never changes. It is still: *Believe Him, obey Him and He will bless you.* Those outstretched arms of Jesus will save all the faithful from Eden to the End of Time.

To read about Noah and the Gopher Tree, Abraham under the Oak at Mamre and Elijah visited by an Angel under a Juniper Tree makes very exciting reading and strengthens the faith of God's people everywhere. Trees played an important part in God's dealings with men. Time and space did not permit a study in this lesson of all the trees mentioned in the Bible. The reader can probably think of other trees that hold a special place in her heart.

The Tree that Became a Cross

I am a tree. I stand proud and tall.
I put forth leaves in Spring and shed them in the Fall.

For years I watched as my fellow-trees were hewn
Some used for shelter, some for warmth but all consumed.

Yet for some reason the Woodman always passed me by,Until
one dark and stormy day I seemed to catch his eye.

I said to this gentle Woodman, "I too want to help mankind."
He replied, "You are the tree I've searched for, for a long time."

Soon the Woodman's axe began to slowly chop away;
Gently he chopped throughout the day.

He checked his blueprint: "Cut one piece short and one long,
Then bind them together and be sure to make it strong!"

"This is a cross. It can't help mankind" he said with a sigh,
"Crosses are made for men who are condemned to die!"

I said to him, "Don't be sad, you only did your duty."
How could he know that cross would turn into sacred beauty?

Upon this cross a mystery will be revealed;
A mystery that from Eternity has been sealed.

I was a tree. I no longer stand tall, but I stand proud.
I hold a blood-stained Lamb before a howling crowd.

A Lamb who counts it all joy to give His life
To save mankind from Satan — save him from sin and strife.

I was a tree — a graceful tree. I became a rugged cross;
A symbol of shame, yet it brought hope for the lost.

When all my fellow-trees are dead and gone
My cross will live in memory, through word and song.

— Farris (Fairy) Parker

THE TREE OF LIFE.:

From the saddest tree in the Bible we turn to the happiest tree — the Tree of Life, which is in "the midst of the Paradise of God" (Revelation 2:7).

In the Revelation of Christ to John, chapter twenty-two, verse two, we can read about this Tree of Life. It is standing on "this side" and on "that side" of the River flowing from the Throne of God and the Lamb. We would say "it stands astride the river." The Tree of Life is an ever-bearing fruit tree, and its leaves are for "the healing of the nations." Nations, plural. All people of all races will benefit:

> Blessed are they that wash their robes, that they may have the right to come to the tree of life ... Revelation 22:14.

We can be assured of these things because Jesus says in verse sixteen, "I Jesus have sent mine angel to testify unto you these things ..."

CONCLUSION

It seems almost inappropriate to bring up a negative thought after reading of the wonders of the Tree of Life in God's beautiful garden, but Jesus himself followed the promise of hope and happiness with a stern warning in the very last paragraph of the last book of the Bible. Read it for yourself; read it carefully and fearfully. In substance, He says that any one who adds to or takes from the words of "this book" will be punished. "God shall take away his part from the tree of life."

God's law hasn't changed from Genesis through Revelation! "Believe Him, obey Him and He will bless you." If one wants to be assured that he has the "right to the Tree of Life" he has only to remember and obey His simple basic law, for *GOD KEEPS HIS WORD.*

> Blessed is the man that walketh not in the counsel of the wicked ... his delight is in the law of Jehovah ... and he shall be like a tree planted by the streams of water, that bringeth forth its fruit in its season ... (Psalm 1:1-3).

I agree with Joyce Kilmer: "I think that I shall never see a poem as lovely as a tree ..."

A PRAYER OF THANKSGIVING

Our Father who art in heaven, Hallowed by thy name.

Thank You for trees. Thank You for the Tree of Life that awaits all the faithful of all ages. Help us to abide in your Word, to believe You and obey You so we through Your grace can live forever with You, Christ, the Holy Spirit and all the redeemed.

Thank You, Father, for the earth that You created for us and help us to be more aware of our duty to take care of it — especially your *Trees*.

We offer this prayer to You in the name of Christ, Redeemer of man, who died on a Tree. Thank You, Lord, for Trees!

Faithfully Yours,
Farris

THINK ON THESE THINGS

1. Trees play an important role in the ecology.

   How?____

   ____

2. What can we (as individuals) do to help preserve trees?

   ____

   ____

3. What is your "favorite tree" of the Bible?___________________

4. Study the graph below to help get a better "time frame" of events in
   the Bible. Ponder the number of years between major events and
   think of the changes in cultures; think of these people as REAL
   people, not as characters in a "good book." Many of these people
   are among "the redeemed of all ages" with whom we will spend
   eternity.

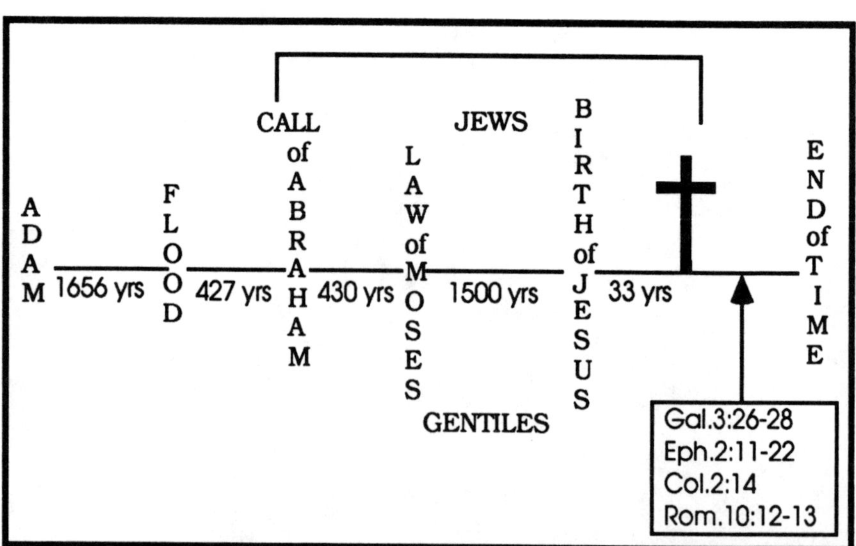

Chapter Five

Face to Face

For now we see in a mirror dimly, but then face to face

(1 Corinthians 13:12).

Faces! How we adore the faces of those we love — mother, father, husband, wife, child and friend. We are overjoyed by their faces.

The faces of those just met or known only slightly are interesting to us, but they can never mean as much as the faces of our loved ones. To us, their faces are the dearest and most beautiful faces in the world.

I love my husband's and children's faces. When far away from them, I experience a deep homesickness to see and touch their faces.

To alleviate this longing, I bring out my collection of snapshots and gaze upon their images. I may even bore others by showing endless pictures of the dearest on earth to me.

A person's face reveals so much about him. Personality, character and temperament can be seen. Often the expression on a person's face reveals what is inside. One can almost read the story of another's life by studying his or her face. Sadness, frustration, joy, contentment, anger, guilt, humor and many other emotions are written clearly on a person's face.

IT'S IN YOUR FACE.

You don't have to tell how you live each day;
You don't have to say if you work or play,
A tried, true barometer serves in the place
However you live, it will show in your face.
The false, the deceit you bear in your heart
Will not stay inside, where it first got a start,
For sinew and blood are a thin veil of lace,
What you wear in your heart you wear in your face.
If your life is unselfish, if for others you live
For not what you get, but how much you can give,
If you live close to God, in His infinite grace,
You don't have to tell it, it shows in your face.

—Author Unknown

TO SEEK HIS FACE

One descriptive phrase in God's Word has always intrigued me. It is the expression, "to seek His face."

David wrote a beautiful Psalm which is recorded in 1 Chronicles 16:10 and 11:

> Let the hearts of those rejoice who seek the
> Lord!   Seek the Lord and His strength;   Seek
> His face evermore!

David's ultimate desire was to gaze upon the beauty of the Lord. From the depths of a longing heart he wrote:

> One thing I have desired of the Lord,
> That will I seek:
> That I may dwell in the house of the Lord
> All the days of my life,
> To behold the beauty of the Lord,
> And to inquire in His temple.
>
> (Psalm 27:4)

Then David added in verses 8 and 9:

> When you said, "Seek My face,"
> My heart said to You, "Your face,
> Lord, I will seek."
> Do not hide Your face from me.

Essentially David was saying, "In Your presence is fullness of joy; at Your right hand are pleasures forevermore" (Psalm 16:11). To seek the Lord's face is to be admitted into His presence.

Many times in the Bible, the word "face" is synonymous with the words "person" or "presence." After Adam and Eve had sinned, they fled "from the presence [literally "from the face" of the Lord,] (Genesis 3:8).

Jesus told His disciples to "seek first the kingdom of God and His righteousness" and everything else would be added. I want to take this admonition seriously for I want to please my heavenly King. It's a wondrous thing to know that day by day we Christians are invited into His presence. In Hebrews 4:16 we are told:

> Let us come boldly to the throne of grace, that we may
> obtain mercy and find grace to help in time of need.

> Let us arise early each morning, eager to "Seek the Lord
> and His strength; seek His face evermore" (Psalm 105:4).

> Every morning lean thine arms awhile
> Upon the window-sill of heaven
> And gaze upon thy Lord,
> Then, with the vision in thy heart,
> Turn strong to meet thy day.
> > — Author Unknown

FACE TO FACE

All through the Bible we read of men and women seeking to view the face of God in all His glory. Not only did they desire His spiritual presence, they longed to see Him "face to face" in His completeness.

Jacob thought he had seen God face to face after he had wrestled all night with an angel. Jacob told him he would not let him go until he had blessed him. He persevered until the blessing was given.

Jacob then called the place "Peniel" which means "face of God." Jacob joyfully exclaimed: "For I have seen God face to face and my life is preserved."

We have no way of knowing why Jacob thought this was truly God, but one thing we do know is that Jacob could not have seen the "fullness of God." The Bible states in several places that no man has ever seen God's face and lived.

In Old Testament times it was dangerous to look fully upon God. It was true then and now, that looking upon God's face is impossible. We cannot look upon His limitless face — His effulgence.

Paul wrote in 1 Timothy 6:16 that God dwells in "unapproachable light." He goes on to say, "whom no man has seen or can see, to whom be honor and everlasting power."

God's glory and light, so brilliant, so dazzling, so bright, is called "unapproachable light." Just as it is dangerous to look into the full face of the sun, so it is out of the question to look "full in His wonderful face" until that day!

John affirmed in John 1:18: "No man has seen God at any time." John 6:46 and 1 John 4:12 state the same truth.

FRIEND WITH FRIEND

This brings us to Exodus 33. The Israelites had grievously sinned against God. They molded and worshiped a golden calf. As a result, God's wrath was kindled against His people. He told them He would send His angel to guide them into the promised land, but He, Himself, would not go with them . . . "lest I consume you on the way." God was being very merciful to let them live at all.

Moses, God's appointed leader, had a very special relationship with Him. Time and again, throughout the Scriptures, we are made aware of the genuine regard God had for Moses. He had been speaking with Moses intimately since the day His presence burst upon Moses from the burning bush.

Verse 11 in this chapter is very significant:

> So the Lord spoke to Moses face to face as a man speaks
> to his friend.

When one speaks "face to face" with someone, we know what that means. We are present to each other — we stand close to one another. We look into each other's eyes as we converse. The children of Israel were cognizant of the special relationship between God and Moses. They told Moses:

> You go near and hear all that the Lord our God may say,
> and tell us all that the Lord our God says to you and we
> will hear and do it (Deuteronomy 5:27).

The Lord said to Moses:

> I have heard the voice of the words of this people which
> they have spoken to you. They are right in all they have
> spoken . . . Go and say to them, "Return to your tents."
> But as for you, stand here by Me, . . ." (Deuteronomy
> 5:28—31).

The Israelites urged Moses to "go near the Lord," while the Lord commanded Moses . . . "stand here by Me."

The close relationship which Moses had with God is something for which we all long. How wonderful to stand by Him, hear what He has to say (through His Word) and to tell others "what great things the Lord has done for us."

THE EYES OF FAITH

Have you ever wondered, as I have, how it could be said that "The Lord spoke to Moses face to face?" We understand the statement, "as a man speaks to his friend," but the part that puzzles us is that they spoke "face to face."

The source of our quandary is found in verse 20:

> But He (God) said, "You cannot see my face; for no man
> shall see Me, and live."

This is the part we do not understand. In the light of God's statement that no man shall see Him and live, how was it possible for the Lord to speak to Moses face to face?"

We also wonder about Jacob (Genesis 32:30); Abraham (Genesis 18:1); Ezekiel (1:1), and Isaiah (6:1). These men were said to have seen God. From Paul's and John's statements we must conclude that these men saw God partially and incompletely.

God is Spirit. He has no body. Yet they saw enough of His glory to be overwhelmed and forever changed by the sight.

I believe Moses saw God "face to face" through the eyes of faith. Hebrews 11:27 compels us to believe this:

> By faith he (Moses) forsook Egypt, not fearing the wrath of the King; for he endured as *seeing Him who is invisible* (emphasis mine).

Moses walked by faith and not by sight. The definition of faith as given in Hebrews 11:1 helps clarify our thinking:

> Now faith is the substance of things hoped for, the evidence of *things not seen.* (emphasis mine).

Faith is seeing invisible things with the eyesight of trust and confidence:

> While we do not look at the things which are seen, but at the things which are not seen. For the things which are seen are temporary, but the things which are not seen are eternal (2 Corinthians 4:18).

Even though God is invisible, Moses could see His face through the gaze of love and faith. David saw God in much the same way:

> As for me, I will see your face in righteousness, I shall be satisfied when I awake in your likeness (Psalm 17:15).

I KNOW

I know I've never seen the wind,
Yet surely it is there,
And who would doubt the fragrance real
We find in springtime air.

So surely when I speak of God,
My heart is all aglow,
I've never seen Him face to face,
And yet He's there — I know.

— Garnett Ann Schultz

Paul wrote a beautiful tribute comparing the physical eye with the spiritual eye which is ours by inheritance:

> Eye has not seen, nor ear heard, Nor have entered into
> the heart of man The things which God has prepared
> for those who love Him (1 Corinthians 2:9).

GOD'S PRESENCE

Returning to the 12th verse of Exodus 33, we find Moses pleading in behalf of the people and himself. He is not happy with the idea that God is only sending an angel with them as they cross over into the land. He pleads for God alone.

In this plea, we find Moses praying for three things:

> That God will show the way.
> That Moses may know Him.
> That he might find grace in God's sight.

"Incidentally," Moses adds, "Don't forget these are *Your people!*"
(I have paraphrased this). Moses feels that His friendship with God entitles him to speak this way.

In verse 14, we find God responding with a tremendous promise:

"MY PRESENCE WILL GO WITH YOU, AND I WILL GIVE YOU REST"

God relented (because of Moses's intercession) and gave the most gracious promise of all time. He, Himself, would go with Moses and the people. He also promised rest — the reward we all wish to obtain after our wilderness wanderings.

God's presence is all we need! Whatever else He may give us, this is our greatest need. To lose the sense of His presence would be our highest loss.

Moses is ecstatic over this reply and states passionately:

> If Your presence does not go with us, do not bring us up
> from here (verse 15).

In other words, "If you are not going with us, we might as well stay right where we are. We cannot make it without Your presence!"

Moses then dared to speak his heart. In this request, He echoes the cry of us all:

> "Please show me Your glory."

This hope, this longing, pulls at our heart strings. You and I want to see the full glory of God's face!

Because we love Him more than anyone on earth, because He is so dear and beloved, because we need Him so much, we want to gaze upon His face! It is only natural for a Father's children to want to see their Father's face. We are homesick for Him.

YOU CANNOT SEE MY FACE

God had been seen in the pillar of cloud by day and the pillar of fire by night. His presence was near when His people met in the tabernacle. His shining glory (Shekinah) was manifested in the temple. Still there was a personal need, especially in Moses, to see God's true, full and complete glory.

It was the deepest need of his heart.

God gently told Moses:

> I will make all My goodness pass before you, and I will proclaim the name of the Lord before you. I will be gracious to whom I will be gracious, and I will have compassion on whom I will have compassion.
> But He said, "You cannot see My face; for no man shall see Me, and live" (Exodus 33:19 and 20).

The Hebrew word for "goodness" means "excellence." God mentions His goodness, His grace and His compassion . . . His most outstanding attributes. He said He would freely give these to Moses and the people but He could not show Moses His face.

It must have been a blow for Moses to hear these words from His dearest friend . . . the One who had walked and talked with Him all these years.

It touches my heart to read the next few verses:

> And the Lord said, "Here is a place by Me, and you shall stand by Me, and you shall stand on the rock. So it shall be, while My glory passes by, that I will put you in the cleft of the rock, and will cover you with My hand while I pass by. Then I will take away My hand, and you shall see My back; but My face shall not be seen" (verses 21-23).

This is what God says to us all. "Here is a place by Me, and you shall stand on the rock." What does the rock signify? It is the place . . . where we are present with Him! You may have heard the expression, "between a rock and a hard place." There are going to be many "rocks" throughout our lifetime, but He is "with us" wherever we stand. God cannot allow us to see His wonderful face in this life. He wants us "to see by faith" during our sojourn here on earth. This does not mean He has withdrawn His presence from us (as He did temporarily with Israel). Moses's plea caused Jehovah God to change His mind and return His presence to His chosen people. To us, as well as to them, He says:

"My Presence will go with you, and I will give you rest."

God says to His personal people in Isaiah 54:7 and 8:

"For a mere moment I have forsaken you,
But with great mercies I will gather you.
With a little wrath I hid my face from you for a moment;
But with everlasting kindness I will have mercy on you,"
Says the Lord, your Redeemer.

SHINING FACES

Another wonderful evidence of God's gracious presence is seen in the glow of His shining face upon us:

The Lord bless you and keep you;
The Lord make His face shine upon you,
And be gracious to you;
The Lord lift up His countenance upon you,
And give you peace (Numbers 6:24-26).

David, calling himself God's servant, pleaded for God's face to shine upon Him in Psalm 31:16 and numerous other places in his Psalms. It was a favorite theme.

A person's face is sometimes reflected in the eyes of the one with whom we are speaking. I have often wondered at this. Just being with the Lord can leave a brilliant impression on our faces. In Lloyd C. Douglas's book, *The Robe*, he has Zacchaeus saying to Jesus, "I saw mirrored in your eyes the kind of man you wanted me to be."

Of course we know that is not a Biblical statement, but from the account in Luke 19, we grasp the impression which Jesus made on Zacchaeus. Do we, as His very own, look into the mirror of His Word often enough to behold Him, so that we shall be like Him?

LIFT UP YOUR EYES

We need to take time from our busy schedules to "lift up our eyes" and look upon Jesus. A definite change will come about in those moments when we look upon His glory.

Isaiah 60:4 and 5 tells us:

> Lift up your eyes all around and see: . . . Then you shall
> see and become radiant, and your heart shall swell with
> joy . . .

In my devotional book *New Day Dawning,* I wrote:

> Every morning what a joy it is to "lift up your eyes and
> look around and see." Whom do we see? Christ Jesus,
> our Lord. "He's here in plain view" as the song goes.
> He's here in this very room!
> This Scripture tells us the happy outcome of looking to
> Him will be that we shall become *radiant.* Psalm 34:5
> repeats this promise: "They looked to Him and were
> radiant, and their faces were not ashamed."
> What does it mean to be radiant? It means we shall
> shine from *within.* It is an inner glow. The radiance
> which shines from our hearts must come from the
> presence of Christ within. The only way any of us can
> shine is to have Christ in our thoughts . . . mind, soul
> and spirit.
> "He has endowed you with splendor " Isaiah 60:9 (NIV)
> tells us. Too many of us have imprisoned our splendor.
> Splendor is brightness which needs to be expended.

God's presence causes a beautiful glow to be seen on our faces.
Just as people realized Peter and John "had been with Jesus," so can
others detect when we have spent time in His presence.

> Not merely in the words you say,
>   Not in your deeds confessed,
> But in the most unconscious way
>   Is Christ expressed.
> Is it a beatific smile?
>   A holy light upon your brow?
> Oh no! I felt His presence while
>   You laughed just now.
> For me 'twas not the truth you taught
>   To you so clear, to me so dim,
> But when you came to me you brought
>   A sense of Him.
> And from your eyes He beckons me,
>   And from your heart His love is shed
> Till I lose sight of you — and see
>   The Christ instead.
>   — Leslie Weatherhead

THE VEIL

In the 34th chapter of Exodus, we see Moses coming down from Mount Sinai with the ten commandments. He has spent 40 days and nights in the presence of God.

We see him walking toward his brother Aaron and the Israelites. They fall back, frightened and bewildered. What has happened to Moses's face?

His face dazzles them with its brilliant radiance. The remarkable thing is that Moses does not know his face is shining!

For awhile, Moses speaks to the people and presents God's commandments as given to him on the mount. After he finishes speaking with them, he covers his face with a veil!

Each time he goes in to speak with the Lord, he takes the veil off, and comes back to the people with fresh shining! Verse 35 tells us:

> And whenever the children of Israel saw the face of Moses, that the skin of Moses's face shone, then Moses would put the veil on his face again, until he went in to speak with Him.

LOOKING TO JESUS

In a great discourse about Moses found in 2 Corinthians 3, we find an explanation of why Moses covered his face with a veil after he came from the presence of God:

> But if the ministry of death, written and engraved on stones, was glorious, so that the children of Israel could not look steadily at the face of Moses because of the glory of his countenance, which glory was passing away, how will the ministry of the Spirit not be more glorious? For if the ministry of condemnation had glory, the ministry of righteousness exceeds much more in glory. For even what was made glorious had no glory in this respect, because of the glory that excels. For if what is passing away was glorious, what remains is much more glorious. Therefore, since we have such hope, we use great boldness of speech — unlike Moses, who put a veil over his face so that the children of Israel could not look steadily at the end of what was passing away. But their minds were hardened. For until this day the same veil remains unlifted in the reading of the Old Testament, because the veil is taken away in Christ.

The more we stay in His glorious presence, the more we look to Jesus, the sooner we'll be changed into His image. Our faces will become like His.

> But we all, with unveiled face, beholding as in a mirror the glory of the Lord, are being transformed into the same image from glory to glory, just as by the Spirit of the Lord (2 Corinthians 3:18).

GOD'S SUNSHINE

Never once since the world began
   Has the sun ever stopped his shining.
His face very often we could not see,
   And we grumbled at his inconstancy;
But the clouds were really to blame, not he
   For behind them, He was shining.

And so — behind life's darkest clouds
   God's love is always shining.
We veil it at times with our faithless fears,
   And darken our sight with our foolish tears,
But in time the atmosphere always clears,
   For His love is always shining.

— John Oxenham

HIS GLORY

In Isaiah 60:2 we are told:

> . . . but the Lord will arise over you, and His glory will be seen upon you (Isaiah 60:2).

How can God's glory be seen upon His people? How can this be? It happens when His people appropriate His glory. We shine because He has shone into our hearts.

> For it is the God who commanded light to shine out of darkness who has shone in our hearts to give the light of the knowledge of the glory of God in the face of Jesus Christ (2 Corinthians 4:6).

The face of Jesus Christ! There is little information in the Bible about the physical appearance of our Lord. We are told in Isaiah 53:2 that He "has no form or comeliness; and when we see Him, there is no beauty that we should desire Him." Yet the Psalmist ascribes to Him these attributes in Psalm 45:2, "You are fairer than the sons of men; Grace is poured upon your lips."

When Paul was speaking of "the face of Jesus Christ" he was describing not His appearance, but His character. "The glory of God in the face of Jesus Christ" is a divine imperative which impresses us to the depths of our being. "And His glory will be seen upon *you*."

How satisfying to realize this is not a passing glory (like the glory of Moses fading away after he came down from the presence of God. This glory can rise upon us morning after morning. (Excerpt from *New Day Dawning*.)

> "It is a curious thing," said an embalmer as he stood by a woman's casket, "but it isn't necessary to tell me she was a Christian. I always know as soon as I see a body; the glory leaves its stamp on the face." (From *New Day Dawning*)
>
> — Author Unknown

> A Japanese lady called to see the headmistress of a mission school. "Do you take only beautiful girls in your school?" she inquired. "Why no; we welcome all girls," was the reply. "But I have noticed that all your girls are beautiful,"said the woman.
> "Well," said the missionary, "we teach them to love our Savior, Jesus Christ, and He gives them a look of beauty."
> "I myself am a Buddhist, and I do not desire my daughter to become a Christian; yet I should like her to attend your school to get that look on her face," was the reply.
>
> — Author Unknown (*New Day Dawning*)

SOMETHING OF THY GLORY

> I would be like thee, blessed Lord and Master,
> That men beholding me may ever trace
> Thy image there — with something of Thy glory
> Clear in my eyes and shining on my face.
>
> — Author Unknown

THE DIM MIRROR

> For now we see in a mirror, dimly, but then face to face.
> Now I know in part, but then I shall know just as I also
> am known (1 Corinthians 13:12).

Someday we shall see His face and know Him perfectly and clearly as God knows and sees us now. The best is yet to be. The most thrilling promise of all is found in 1 John 3:2,

Beloved, now we are children of God; and it has not yet been revealed what we shall be, but we know that when He is revealed, we shall be like Him, for we shall see Him as He is.

FACE TO FACE

Face to face with Christ my Savior,
Face to face — what will it be,
When with rapture I behold Him,
Jesus Christ who died for me?

Only faintly now I see him
With the darkling veil between;
But a blessed day is coming,
When His glory shall be seen.

What rejoicing in His presence,
When are banished grief and pain,
But a blessed day is coming,
When His glory shall be seen.

Face to face! O blissful moment!
Face to face — to see and know;
Face to face with My Redeemer,
Jesus Christ, who loves me so.

Chorus:
Face to face shall I behold Him,
Far beyond the starry sky; . . .
Face to face, in all His glory,
I shall see Him by and by.

— Mrs. Frank A. Breck and Grant Colfax Tullar

Ethelyn Mitchell wrote:

Let the beauty and peace of God fall upon our brow and it will speak God's eternal message to all who gaze upon it.

Father in heaven, Oh, that we might capture Thy glory and light the first thing in the morning, that we might carry it with us all through the day. May we have Thy glory stamped on our faces. In Jesus's Name, Amen.

Faithfully Yours,
Judy Miller

THINK ON THESE THINGS

1. Why is a person's face so important?

2. What was David's ultimate desire?

3. The word "face" in the Bible is synonymous with the words _____or ______ .

4. After Jacob wrestled with the angel, what name did he give that place? What does that name mean?

5. What does it mean to speak "face to face" with a person?

6. How did Moses see God "face to face?"

7. What does the word *faith* mean?

8. If you were to give a title to Exodus 33, what would it be?

9. When we speak of "the rock" what do we mean?

10. David pleaded for ______ _____ ___ _______ ____ _____ in Psalm 31:16.

11. What does it mean to be radiant?

12. Why did Moses cover his face with a veil after returning from the presence of God?

13. How can God's glory be seen upon His people?

14. Memorize 1 John 3:2 today and share it with another.

Chapter Six

Relationships In Life—Part I

INTRODUCTION: The purpose of this lesson, and the aim of the writer is to show the *ideal* relationship between husband and wife. If you, dear reader, feel you cannot measure up to this standard, then you are *in the majority.* Although God does not expect His children to be perfect, He does expect them to continually strive to be their best.

I. THE DIVINE SPARK:

True happiness for a woman often emanates from her good relationship with her husband. Likewise, true happiness for both husband and wife results from their good relationship with God, Christ and the church.

Jehovah said in Genesis 2:18, "It is not good for man to be alone, I will make him a help meet for him." The word *meet* here is defined "worthy"or "suitable." In our everyday speech we may say: "I will make for him a worthy companion."

From all the beautiful and perfect animals that God had made (and Adam had named) there was not one found suitable for Adam. Animals are physical beings *only,* while man is a living soul made in the image of his Maker, God. Animals live and die. Mankind, however, lives forever. None of the magnificent animals formed out of the ground had that spark of Divinity that Elohim had breathed into Adam.

God determined to make someone special for Adam — someone *right* for man — so perfect that he would be complete. God made someone so completely *right for man* that there would be no void in his life. He made someone worthy of the Divine Spirit in man and someone with whom he could reproduce after his own kind. He made her *from* man and *for* man. She was neither superior nor inferior to man. God made her to be Adam's wife! "And the man called his wife's name Eve . . ." (Genesis 3:20).

When God made Eve, He caused a deep sleep to fall upon Adam and from his side took a bone to make her. God could have created her out of the ground as He had created Adam, but then she would have been a separate entity — a distinct being to whom man would have no physical tie. But God formed her out of the same flesh and bone taken from Adam. Genesis 2:22,23 gives this account:

> The rib, which Jehovah God had taken from the man,
> made he a woman, and brought her unto the man. And
> the man said, This is now bone of my bones, and flesh
> of my flesh: she shall be called Woman, because she
> was taken out of Man.

The Hebrew word "woman" is translated "she-man" or "man-with-a-womb." Woman is equal to man intellectually and spiritually; physically she is said to be the "weaker vessel" (1 Peter 3:7).

II. THEY SHALL BE ONE:

"No happiness is like unto it, No love so great, As that of man and wife." This quotation is found on pieces of needlepoint, wall plaques and other objects given for wedding anniversary gifts, especially for fifty and over years of marriage.

God's word reveals the source of this happiness in Genesis 2:24:

> Therefore shall a man leave his father and his mother,
> and shall cleave unto his wife: and they shall be one
> flesh.

This command does not imply that a man stop loving, respecting and caring for his parents.

The Apostle Paul adds that the relationship between husband and wife must be like that between Christ and His Church (Ephesians 5:25). Today's flippant attitude toward the sacred vows of marriage is depressing. Sons and daughters should be taught that the relationship between husband and wife exists until one dies. They also should continually be reminded that their relationship to God will depend to a great degree upon their fidelity toward their mates. Parents would do well to read the traditional marriage vows to their children even before they start dating. Many married couples have never heard these solemn vows given before God until they themselves give them at their own marriage. Too often couples forget that part of their vows is "until death do us part."

III. WIVES DIVINELY COMMISSIONED:

When governments appoint ambassadors to another country, those ambassadors function in the particular area to which they are assigned. They are not to invade another's field of service, but can help only when called upon to do so. In a similar way the Holy Spirit has given women a certain sphere in which to function. For example, a wife must stay within the confines of her area in order to please God and allow the Holy Spirit to direct her life.

One contributing factor to the moral decay of the American home is a woman's neglect to maintain a proper home environment for her family. Her Divine Commission is to be a keeper of the home. The primary meaning of this command is to see that her family has nourishing food, proper clothing and a quiet, clean house to which they can retreat from the pressures of the day, along with lots of TLC (tender loving care). But there is more!

> Speak thou the things which befit the sound doctrine . . . that aged women . . . train the young women to love their husbands, to love their children . . . to be workers at home, kind, being in subjection to their own husbands, that the word of God be not blasphemed (Titus 2:1-5).

The fact that a young wife is to be *taught* to love her husband is evidence that love for him must be more than infatuation. Loving a husband means cherishing him *in spite* of his faults; it means respecting him and being in subjection to him.

The thought that a mother must be *taught* to love her children seems absurd, doesn't it? Yet, there is more to being a mother than giving physical birth. Even animals reproduce! Among other things, loving children includes using discipline when necessary.

Real love for one's children is to teach them God's truths in order that their souls will be saved. It means training them to develop into good citizens of their school, neighborhood and country. Most important, however, is to teach them to become good citizens in God's Kingdom. In view of all this, it is clear that this teaching should begin early at home. Often it is too late when parents wait until the "young woman" marries and has children of her own.

The Apostle Paul certainly taught that older women should teach the younger. This teaching should not be confined to a class room. All mothers are older than their daughters and come under the classification of "older women" who should assume this responsibility. Waiting for some other older women to teach these precious souls in a Bible class room is shirking her divine commission.

It is a shame to her husband and a dishonor to her God when a wife undermines her husband's position as head of the family. The Holy Spirit states this principle a little stronger. He says she is guilty of "blasphemy" if she does not ascribe the proper authority to her husband (Titus 2:5).

Some people think it is amusing when movies, cartoons and TV shows depict the husband and father as a stumbling, bumbling Mr. Milquetoast sort of a man. The wife and children always appear smarter and the man of the house appears to be a "wimp".

This point was illustrated in a newspaper cartoon. Two women were shown talking over the back fence. One said: "My husband makes all the decisions at our house. All I do is accept them or reject them." That is not what the Holy Spirit had in mind when He said, "Wives, be in subjection unto your own husbands . . . for the husband is the head of the wife . . ." (Ephesians 5:22,23).

My dear friend, Donna Horne, wrote in her book *Meanwhile, Back in the Jungle*, page 56.

> By the way, it is literally true that every African man is
> the head of his wife. In public gatherings he sits ahead
> of his wife; in the home he eats ahead of his wife, and
> along the foot trails he always walks ahead of his wife.

NEITHER IS *THAT* WHAT THE HOLY SPIRIT HAD IN MIND! (Ephesians 5:25).

The attitude of submission must be right. Many women are submissive to their husbands because they are forced to be. Some are afraid. If they are coerced into subjection they may do so with rebellion in their hearts. Prisoners of war are subject to their guards. Inmates are subject to the warden, *but not willingly.* A school teacher told of one of her students who was so hyper that she had trouble keeping him in his seat. Finally, she became exasperated and *forced* him to sit, with the stern command, "Now you sit there!" With a belligerent look he said, "You think I'm sitting, but inside I'm standing." Submission (and obedience) must be done willingly and in love. That is God's way.

All these things are idealistic. We hear a chorus of voices from women of all ages and from all walks of life: "I must live in the real world; I must cope with situations that are less than ideal! Can I be true to myself — be my own person — and still submit to another?"

No one has all the answers, nor do they presume to know all the problems of the Christian woman of today — how she is struggling to be a good wife and mother, and in some cases having to act as both mother and father.

One possible solution to the problems would be for the church to start ongoing classes for husbands and fathers to help them cope with *their* problems. This could have a profound effect upon the men involved and also upon their families. This class should be more than a six-weeks course, and should be taught on a regular schedule. It would help men to be better husbands, fathers and Christians. With enough interest it could be a permanent class in the education program. Women who have been teaching "Ladies' Bible Classes" for years hear over and over from young women attending these classes: "Why doesn't someone tell *that* to my husband? Why isn't there a class for husbands similar to our class for wives?"

IV. GOD'S DIVINE PLACE FOR MEN IN THE HOME:

The husband is to be head of the home (Ephesians 5:23). The awesome responsibility of parents to teach their children "the way of the Lord" rightly rests largely upon the father. In many cases, however, the mother must assume this duty because the father is not functioning in his designated area. The wife should encourage her husband to recognize and carry out his God-given duty by cooperating with him and teaching the children that his authority must be obeyed.

Submission of a wife to her husband as head of the home will be easier when the husband earns that respect.

V. PLATEAUS OF LIFE:

Relationships may be on different plateaus because of age and/or circumstances. It is hoped that the following discussions on a variety of categories will be helpful:

> 1. Brides
> 2. Young Mothers
> 3. Wife of a non-Christian Husband

In Part 2 of this lesson we will discuss: *The Working Wife; The Barren Wife; Teachers;* and *Wives of Preachers and Elders.*

A. BRIDES:

There are many adjustments for a bride! Every married woman was at first a bride. She and her new husband had some "getting used to" in their new relationship.

The bride and her husband might have come from different backgrounds, different environments and sometimes different levels of education.

The moment the bride says "I do" she instantly acquires in-laws. She discovers that she has married a family as well as a husband. Perhaps his family's ways and customs are different from hers. Maybe her in-laws' religious beliefs are different or even foreign to hers. This can be a big challenge for a young bride. She often must walk a fine line in dealing with this situation. She must be courteous, but consistent and uncompromising in her loyalty and service to God.

In the same instant that the bride acquired in-laws, she also became an in-law. Her husband has married a family as well as a wife. This is one of the real life situations with which she must deal. The best rule to follow is the Golden Rule. This rule or measuring rod can be used to measure the importance of all problems and help in making proper decisions. It will help the couple to find the length, width and depth of the consequences!

Often the bride must move literally hundreds of miles away from family and friends. Money problems may arise. Perhaps her husband may need to gain years of experience on his job before he can give her the material things to which she was accustomed. One bride of a few months said that she solved this problem by going shopping. *SHOPPING?* Yes, "window shopping" and looking at all the beautiful things she could do without!

B. YOUNG MOTHERS:

With the arrival of children the relationship of husband and wife is extended. It is now *father, mother* and child.

The mood and tone of the home is often set by the wife and mother. She is indeed the "keeper" of the home (Titus 2:5).; She is the keeper of unity, orderliness and stability. The mother becomes the "keeper" of peace at the risk of being a go-between and finding herself "in the middle" — a buffer. A buffer smooths things out! Jesus said in Matthew 5:14-16:

> Ye are the light of the world . . . so let your light shine
> before men; that they may see your good works, and
> glorify your Father who is in heaven.

Mother, you are a light in your home. Let's paraphrase the above passage and substitute the letter "I" for the word *you.*

> *I* am the light in my home, so *I* will let my light shine
> before my husband and children that they may see my
> good works and glorify our Father who is in heaven.

How many times do wives and mothers get tired and become frustrated, forgetting they have within themselves the power to shape the lives and destinies of those they love? MANY TIMES, if they are average housewives and mothers. Christian wives and mothers must try to remember that they have a unique opportunity not afforded everyone — an opportunity to mold and shape their children before they go out into the world.

Mothers with young children in their care may at some point feel imprisoned within the confines of their home. They may feel "chained" to cooking, cleaning and that ever-present load of clothes to be washed, dried and folded! They should be encouraged to remember the words of the Apostle Paul when *he* was in chains in a Roman prison: "I am an ambassador in chains" (Ephesians 6:20), "but the word of God is not bound" (2 Timothy 2:9).

Paul taught the word of God to those who were chained to him as well as to others who were in prison with him. Mothers can teach their little ones (who are chained to her) as they go about their daily chores. They have a "captive audience!" An average family has three children. A mother of three can be directly responsible for saving three souls for eternity. That may very well be more souls than the same mother could save with unlimited time to go door-to-door trying to save souls. The family unit is in reality a *unit of the church.* Christian mothers should not let "church work" outside the home keep them from doing "church work" inside the home.

Parents should teach their children short memory verses from the Bible. They should take every opportunity to teach them to cultivate good manners, good habits and good thoughts. Children should be taught to respect the authority of their parents; if they do not respect them they will not respect the authority of school teachers or of civil laws, neither will they respect the laws of God.

Parents should not be overly concerned about leaving their children money or property. It is more important to give them something that will sustain them as Christians and will insure them of an *incorruptible inheritance* with Christ and all the redeemed. There are many simple truths that Christian parents can instill into their children. They can be taught to *appreciate the beauty of Calvary; the solemnity of the Lord's Supper; to love the simplicity of the Lord's Church;* to know they can have *a hope of heaven* that will sustain them in trials and even unto death. They can be taught at an early age the beautiful, yet awesome, words of Jesus in Matthew 16:26 (KJV): "For what is a man profited, if he shall gain the whole world and lose his own soul?"

C. THE NON-CHRISTIAN HUSBAND:

Not every Christian wife has a Christian husband (1 Corinthians 7:13-16). Regardless of how a Christian woman got into this relationship, she is there. Perhaps she married before learning the truth and becoming a Christian herself. Perhaps she allowed her heart to rule over her head. When one is young and in love, Christ and His Church sometimes take a back seat. Death is a long way down the road and she has time to think about that later — or so she reasons. At any rate, she is married to a man whom she dearly loves, but one who does not share her religious views.

One's relationship with God does not change with marriage. *This* relationship is eternal. If the husband is not yet a Christian, the wife still owes him the respect due him as her husband and the father of her children. She owes him the honor due him as head of the home and she owes him her undivided love. Paul says:

> The women that hath an unbelieving husband, and he
> is content to dwell with her, let her not leave her
> husband (1 Corinthians 7:13).

Verse sixteen of chapter seven says: "For how knowest thou, O wife, whether thou shalt save thy husband?" The wife will not save him if she is not in subjection to him and does not have the proper relationship with him. Her influence can best be felt by keeping God first in *her* life and functioning in *her* God-given sphere:

> Wives, be in subjection to your own husbands; that,
> even if any obey not the word, they may without the
> word be gained by the behavior of their wives;
> beholding your chaste behavior coupled with fear (1
> Peter 3:1,2).

The woman with a non-Christian husband has special problems and must continually ask the Lord for His guidance. She must be steadfast in the faith, never compromising the truth. Temptation to neglect the assembly is very strong when she must attend alone. She must seek ways of escape from this temptation. "God . . . will not suffer you to be tempted above that ye are able, but will with the temptation make also the way of escape . . ." (1 Corinthians 10:13). She must strive to keep open the line of communication. If they cannot discuss family affairs how can she talk to him about his soul?

The attitude of tolerance cannot be over emphasized. Tolerance is not weakness; it is strength, seeing things with the heart instead of with the eyes. This woman must be careful not to let anxiety over his salvation drive her to being contentious about religious matters. No one is wrong about *everything* in the area of religion. *Even a stopped clock is right twice a day!*

This wife — and all wives — should show the man that she married that he is the most important person in the world to her. *If* he is different from the man she fell in love with and married, has she helped to make him different? Is the change for the better?

The Christian wife of a yet-to-be-Christian must guard her tongue. "Death and life are in the power of the tongue" (Proverbs 18:21). She should never "put her husband down" or tell others of his shortcomings. When he does become a Christian other people will know only his good qualities. His wife must be patient, going time and again to her inner closet and asking God to help her say the *right* things. *Doors of communication can be closed by saying the* wrong *things.*

The Martyr Complex is one of the hardest problems with which to deal. A wife in this position may find herself saying (hopefully to herself!): "How many more times must I walk out of this house *alone* to go to worship? I go three times a week for regular worship and Bible study, five times in one week to VBS, seven nights to a gospel meeting, once a month to Teachers Meeting. That is almost two hundred nights a year I go alone regardless of weather conditions or how I feel. I prepare an early supper, dress the kids and walk out leaving him in his easy chair reading the evening paper."

"Why should I have all the responsibility of the spiritual training of the children? That is really his duty! Why must I be the only one in my Bible class without a husband sitting beside me? Class parties are no fun when you must go alone. Some people jokingly call me a 'church widow.' I smile, but it is not a laughing matter. Why must *I* make all the efforts and sacrifices? What will it take to convert my husband to Christ?" Answer: *Everything you have!*

It is only human for a Christian wife to ask herself these questions. She has said *to herself* more than once: "I go to class after class taught by godly women married to godly men . . . but what do they know about MY situation? They are not in my shoes!"

She may not be altogether correct about this. There are many women in the Lord's church who have "sat where she sits." They have lived through many years of discouragement and heartache before seeing *their* spouse become a Christian. Some day *this* woman will realize she was being *forged in a furnace of fire*, being molded into a strong, faithful servant of God. The Apostle Peter says it better in 1 Peter 1:6,7:

> Wherein ye greatly rejoice . . . ye have been put to grief in manifold trials, that the proof of your faith, being more precious than gold that perisheth though it is proved by fire, may be found unto praise and glory and honor at the revelation of Jesus Christ.

Gold is pure only after going through the furnace, leaving behind the dross. This woman is building strength, faith and courage although she must often think the opposite. She has at times wondered why God does not answer her prayers and wonders how much longer she can go on. She will come to realize that she is dealing with the *will* of another person; that will cannot be forced to obey God. God, Himself, does not coerce anyone to obey Him. She will come to grips with such scriptures as Ezekiel 33:8,9; Philippians 2:12; and 1 Peter 3:1,2.

Sisters of kindred spirit who have sat where *this* woman sits, tell her: "Remain faithful to the Lord and His church. Do not jeopardize *your* soul by compromising the truth, and *never let your light go out.*" One day, probably when she is least expecting it, her husband may decide for himself to become a Christian and say to her the most wonderful words she will ever hear: "Honey, I am going to be baptized into Christ." *

As a mother who gives birth to her child soon forgets the pain of birth, so will this wife forget all the heartaches when her husband is "born of water and the Spirit." The angels of heaven will rejoice and her light will shine brighter than ever. *Two* lights in the same house give *twice* as much light as one! She can *then* say with Paul:

> For I reckon that the sufferings of this present time are
> not worthy to be compared with the glory which shall
> be revealed to us-ward (Romans 8:18).

By the Grace of God, through faith, this woman can find strength and assurance that He will bless her efforts. He will "comfort your hearts and establish them in every good work and word" (2 Thessalonians 2:17).

* — The author and her husband were married for thirty-seven years before she saw him baptized into Christ.

Faithfully Yours,
Farris

THINK ON THESE THINGS

1. What is the meaning of the word "meet" in Genesis 2:18?

2. Discuss "keeper of the home" in Titus 2:5.

3. To be submissive, one must have the ________________
   ________________ .

4. Should a Christian wife be in subjection to a non-Christian husband?

5. Memorize Romans 8:18.

6. Discuss at length the following scriptures:

   (a) Ezekiel 33:8,9 ____

   ____

   (b) Philippians 2:12 ______________________________________

   ____

   (c) 1 Peter 3:1,2 ____

   ____

Chapter Seven

Relationships in Life - Part II

I. THE WORKING WIFE:

Some wives apparently must work outside the home. Often such a wife can slip into Satan's trap and begin to assert her independence from her husband. This need not be the case, yet it is difficult to maintain one's balance when thrown into the business world of competition with all its allurements.

The career woman must do a juggling act in order to work both outside and inside the home. She cannot neglect her work or she will lose her job, yet she must not neglect her family or she will lose *them.* She must be strong in order to balance two jobs. She should *take* time for her family. Some say *make* time, but how can one make time? Every person has twenty-four hours in a day and that is all. Time taken from something of less importance and used to strengthen her family would certainly be time well spent!

The working wife is a "light" in her home and can also be a light among her co-workers. It is possible that she is the *only* "light of the world" in her office among her fellow workers.

Working wives (along with women in all walks of life) would do well to ask themselves this soul searching question: "What am I doing now that will count for anything worthwhile a year from now? Five years from now? In eternity?"

Priscilla was a working wife and she accomplished some works that will be counted worthwhile in eternity. She and her husband were tent makers. One can imagine Priscilla adding that "woman's touch" to the tents. Her special touch would surely make them more attractive and appealing to their customers.

One day Priscilla and her husband met a man who also was a tent maker — the Apostle Paul. It is likely that Paul converted this fine couple to Christ. Paul worked with them, lived in their home and through their joint efforts a congregation of the Lord's Church was established in Corinth. The Christians met in the home of Priscilla and Aquilla. The friendship with this working wife and her husband was to give a special dimension to Paul's life. He included these two dear friends in the great book of First Corinthians, chapter 16, verse 19: (KJV)

> The churches of Asia salute you. Aquila and Priscilla
> salute you ... with the church that is in their house.

This Jewish couple had been expelled from Rome, but later they were able to return to their homeland. In writing to the church at Rome, Paul made this wonderful statement:

> Greet Priscilla and Aquila, my fellow workers in Christ
> Jesus.   They risked their lives for me (Romans 16:3
> NIV).

Shortly before his death, Paul wrote: "I have fought the good fight; I have finished the course; I have kept the faith ..." This beautiful passage has been quoted numberless times and is remembered by scholars everywhere — but the words following this poignant statement should also be remembered: "I send greetings to Priscilla and Aquila." This placed a divine stamp of approval on a *working wife* who helped her husband but did not neglect her service to God. At one point she helped her husband teach a young preacher "the way of the Lord more perfectly."

Priscilla was a working wife who went about her everyday living, functioning in the area divinely assigned to women, a true help-mate to her husband who counted her worthy to share in his work. We are not told whether this couple had children.

II. THE BARREN CHRISTIAN:

At this point it seems fitting to speak of the Christian woman who is unable to bear children. For reasons unknown this subject seems to have been avoided in most books designed for ladies' classes.

There are many fine Christian women who are not mothers — either by natural means or by adoption. Before Christ came into the world and restored woman to the position intended for her from the beginning it was a stigma and a disgrace to be childless. This attitude does not seem to prevail under the New Testament law. Today it is a matter of choice for some women — even for some Jewish women who are still looking for the Messiah.

Considering the multitude of unwanted, abused and abandoned children in the world it makes one sad to think of the women, now and in times past, who have been unable to bear children. Fortunately, with modern medical techniques, minor surgery can correct the problem in many cases. It has not always been so and is not always successful even today.

God has a place in His Kingdom for every person! The barren wife, the unmarried lady (by choice), the career woman and those with one or a dozen children. God would have the childless woman give to Him all the talents and energies that would have been expended on a family had the circumstances been different for her.

Some women suffer embarrassing moments and a degree of depression on Mother's Day. In many congregations mothers, grandmothers and great-grandmothers are asked to stand and be recognized. Some pin a rose on each mother as she enters the building. All of this is nice and a Christian mother deserves to be honored. It is hoped that her children will continue to honor her and care for her as long as she lives. It is also hoped that mothers will live in such a way that their children will "rise up and call her blessed."

Among the finest teachers in public schools or in Bible schools are women who have no children of their own. These women seem to be able to teach objectively and to administer discipline impartially. They spend much time, energy and their own money to make their rooms attractive and conducive to better learning. They give that extra part of themselves usually reserved for one's own children.

A mother wrote an article which appeared in a religious paper a few years ago. The "letter" expresses heartfelt love and appreciation for all those non-mothers who have taught numberless children and molded lives into useful citizens. The letter is signed, "A Grateful Mother."

TRIBUTE TO A NON-MOTHER

Sing, O barren, thou that didst not bear; break forth into singing, and cry aloud, thou that didst not travail with child: for more are the children of the desolate than the children of the married wife, saith the Lord. Enlarge the place of thy tent, and let them stretch forth the curtains of thine inhabitations: spare not, lengthen thy cords, and strengthen thy stakes (Isaiah 54:1,2).

Dear Non-Mother:

You dread facing another Mother's Day service; you who have wept, questioned, struggled, prayed and finally accepted your barrenness. Listen to me!
I love and admire you! You could have retreated into self-pity, but you didn't. You could have blamed God, but you didn't. You could have taken your frustration out on others' children — refused to teach their Sunday School class, tie their shoe laces, or lift them up to the drinking fountain — but you didn't. Instead you "enlarged your tent," broadened your vision, and reached out to my child.

You didn't stop there. You "stretched forth the curtains of your habitation" as you encircled other children with your love and time. You thought I didn't notice, but I did.

I heard my child repeat with breathless excitement the stories you told in Sunday School. I saw the sparkle in her eyes and the eagerness in her step as she approached your class each Sunday, and I thanked God for you.

Years have passed, and you continue to minister. I've watched you grow and blossom with an ever expanding love. You've touched the lives of hundreds of little ones — crisp, shiny, clean ones, grubby, wiggly mischievous ones; and still you lengthen your cords and strengthen your stakes.

Every area of the church involved with children has felt the impact of your influence. Your ministry is priceless to the church and to God; you are one of His chosen vessels.

May God bless you, overshadow you, uplift and strengthen and sustain you. This Mother's Day, while others receive special recognition, you can stand tall. No, they won't recognize you as a mother; in fact, they may not notice you at all. But God will notice — for you are special and your children are many.

I Love you.

A Grateful Mother

III. TEACHERS:

Teachers, you are the light in your class room. You are the "light" both academically and morally to your students, whether you teach in a Bible School or in public school. You may be the only true light that some of your students will ever see; the only one to put a loving arm around a neglected child. Your kind words may be the only ones he will hear all day. One never knows the kind of home environment he will return to at the end of day. A seed of kindness you sow could grow into the salvation of his soul. "Let your light shine" before your students that they may see your good works; your Father in heaven will be glorified.

A. If you are a teacher of the Bible you are an important part of the Lord's Church! Many do not realize it, but the Holy Spirit placed teachers in the church along with evangelists and elders:

> And he gave some to be apostles; and some prophets;
> and some evangelists; and some elders and some
> teachers (Ephesians 4:11).

Teachers were placed in the church along with preachers and elders! A congregation can exist without a preacher or without elders (though they should not for long), but a congregation cannot exist without teaching. The Word of God must be taught if Christians are to reproduce and grow. The Word of God is the *seed* for reproducing Christians. As a seed must be planted in soil in order to germinate and bring forth fruit, so must God's Word be planted in the minds of men through teaching.

Unfortunately and for reasons unknown this divine appointment of *teachers* is rarely mentioned, never stressed and often is not known by church members — sometimes not known to teachers themselves. The fact — the little known fact — is that the Holy Spirit placed evangelists, elders *and* teachers in the church. Every Christian teaches in some way — publicly, privately and by example. Not everyone can be a teacher in a class room, but those who do have a very special responsibility to know the truth and to teach it in love. It is an awesome thing to be responsible for "handling aright" the Word of God.

B. Teachers of adult classes perform a special function within the church, instructing and edifying. However, teachers of small children, pre-teens and high school ages have the most influential and rewarding job of all. They are in a unique position to mold the mind of a child who will in his own time stand before God to be judged for eternity. Not only does the teacher mold and shape for eternity but is a powerful influence in the lives of future citizens of our country.

Teachers go about their ways quietly doing what they can to save souls. The hours spent in study and preparation for lessons can be known only to the teacher and to God. *He knows.* These divinely appointed servants of God always appreciate a "thank you" from parents whose children are being molded into useful "earthen vessels" who in time could be teachers!

Seldom are these self-sacrificing workers mentioned in public prayers at worship. Every time a public prayer is offered for the divinely appointed evangelists and elders a similar prayer should be offered for divinely appointed teachers. If this happened more often, perhaps the educational part of the church would reach its potential.

The best reward teachers receive is knowledge gained from intense study. Paul knew this to be true when he said in Romans 2:21: "He who teaches another teaches himself also."

IV. THE OLDER CHRISTIAN:

This may apply to years and in service to the Lord. Older Christians have reached another plateau in life. Perhaps they have suddenly found themselves unable to do the things they were once able to do. They can no longer go at the speed they once maintained *all day*. Perhaps they have a physical disability. Their names no longer appear at the top of the list for volunteers because they have learned they must say "no" to things they would truly like to do. Looking around, they find that everything seems to be geared for the young. But none of this keeps them from doing their best in their service to the Lord. They are at worship services every time it is possible for them to get there and grieved if circumstances keep them away. The church grows dearer to them as they grow older, "for now salvation is nearer to us than when we first believed" (Romans 13:11).

Those Christian women who stood beside their husbands for years, who have been steadfast through adversities, who stand in the "old paths" and refuse to "remove the ancient landmarks" are still glorifying God through their lives and good works.

Those women, along with godly men of past generations, have fought error and stood firm in the face of criticism, and are to some degree responsible for the church of our Lord being where it is today. Many are warming by the fires that they kindled! "O woman, great is thy faith . . ." (Matthew 15:28).

V. A SPECIAL CATEGORY:

The one time active Christian woman (regardless of age) who suddenly finds herself shut off from "church activities" due to an invalid husband, aged parent or a disabled child is in reality doing "church work" in the truest sense. There can be no greater way to glorify God through her life than by caring for her loved ones. This woman is ministering to Christ! Jesus said, "I was sick and you ministered unto me." When asked when they had seen Him sick He replied: "Inasmuch as ye did it unto one of these my brethren, even these least, ye did it unto me" (Matthew 25:40).

In verse 36 of Matthew 25, Jesus said, "I was in prison and ye visited me . . ." This true servant of Christ replies: "I have never in all my life visited *anyone* in prison!" Maybe not *in person*, but you certainly have ministered to some in prison — not imprisoned by brick and iron bars, but imprisoned by loneliness. Remember that casserole you sent to the family imprisoned with grief? Have you forgotten the time you heard of a sister in Christ having marital problems and you invited her over for lunch and counseled with her? You surely haven't forgotten the teenager down the street who was having problems at school passing exams? She came to *you* and you helped her with some math problems; you thought that you had forgotten all about math, but it came back to you when giving of yourself to one in need. You are doing what we like to call "church work" but a better term may be *Christ's work.*

VI. WIVES OF PREACHERS AND ELDERS:

No preacher or elder can function properly in his divinely appointed sphere without the help of a dedicated wife. It is hard to bear the burdens of the spiritually weak without an understanding wife. Preachers and elders spend countless hours in prayer — agonizing over wayward and indifferent members — they need a patient wife! At times they need to unburden their hearts and need a trustworthy companion who will not repeat confidential information.

It takes a dedicated, steadfast and godly man to be a preacher or elder, and it takes a dedicated, steadfast and godly woman to stand behind him, and walk *beside* him. This woman lives in the shadow of her husband yet she must always be there, properly groomed, in a cheerful mood, a smile on her face and ready to do any job required of her. And for some reason church members seem to expect more of them than they do of other women. And they always seem to fulfill that requirement.

"How beautiful are the feet of them who preach the gospel" (Romans 10:15). At the risk of seeming irreverent, it might be said: How beautiful are those who wash the socks, iron the shirts and cook the meals for those who preach the gospel.

CONCLUSION

God's woman has been the focal point in this study of "Life's Relationships." She has been admired, praised and exhorted. She can rightly be compared to *iron, gold and diamonds.*A Christian woman displays the strength of iron by standing for truth and righteousness in a world gone mad with error and immorality. She is pure gold, being refined day by day in a furnace of trials and temptations. She is a diamond, standing out in all its beauty amid sordid things of the world. She enhances her setting with kindness, courage, love and dignity. She is many faceted and stays polished through her service to God until she shines with brightness in a world of darkness. She reflects her light as she moves about in her *divinely appointed* sphere and lets her light shine before others, bringing glory to God who made her. She is man's most prized possession. SHE IS WOMAN!

Faithfully Yours,
Farris

THINK ON THESE THINGS

1. The career wife has _________________ _________________
    in a day.

2. Priscilla and her husband were _____________ ____________
    by trade.

3. In ancient times it was a _____________________ to be
    childless.

4. The _______________ _______________ placed teachers in
    the church.

5. Name three things in 2 Kings 4:26 that should be
    remembered:_______________ _________________
    _______________ .

Chapter Eight

The Changing Power of Christ

And do not be conformed to this world, but be transformed by the renewing of your mind, that you may prove what is that good and acceptable and perfect will of God (Romans 12:2).

One year our Wednesday night Ladies' Bible class had selected the theme, "Attitudes of the Renewed Mind." We used the above verse as a recurring theme. One vital principle was stressed: Until one's mind is renewed, attitudes remain the same.

Is change essential for the Christian's development and growth? As Christians in the process of being less and less conformed to this world, we must also be changing more and more into the image of Christ.

The Christian life is not a stagnant pond, but rather like a river, ever changing as it draws its resources from above. Since "our times are in His hands" we should ever be longing for a deeper change.

CHRIST'S ENABLING POWER

It takes courage to change. It also takes confidence. First, we must have confidence in the Lord and His overwhelming power to change us. Second, we must have confidence in our selves. We *do* have the ability and strength to allow Jesus to change us. Little by little we become more like Him. We are changed into His very image.

Little by Little

Little by little every day
Little by little in every way
Jesus is changing me
       Is changing me.
Since I made a turnabout face
I've been growing in His grace
Jesus is changing me.

He's changing me
My precious Jesus
I'm not the same person
That I used to be.

Sometimes its slow going
But there's a knowing
That someday
Perfect I will be.

— Author Unknown

Werner Erhard said: "You and I possess within ourselves at every moment of our lives, under all circumstances, the power to transform the quality of our lives."

How do we obtain this power? Christ has the power to change our lives to the extent we allow Him. Without Christ's enabling power, neither you nor I can change.

We can withstand this power, yet without it we will remain the same. Jesus can transform and change us when "we let Him have His way with us."

Now, let us think through:

TEN IMPORTANT CONSIDERATIONS IN MAKING CHANGES:

1. RECOGNIZE THE NEED FOR CHANGE

First of all, we need to acknowledge and isolate specific areas which need change and improvement. If we do not recognize these areas, we have no point of reference. Someone has said: "Not everything that is faced can be changed, but nothing can be changed until it is faced."

Pinpointing specific needs will focus our direction. Let us face up to the fact that some changes need to take place.

NEW BEGINNINGS

How often we wish for another chance
To make a fresh beginning
A chance to blot out our mistakes
And change failure into winning
And it does not take a new year
To make a brand new start.
It only takes the deep desire
To try with all our hearts.

To live a little better
And to always be forgiving
And to add a little sunshine
To the world in which we're living.
So never give up in despair
And think that you are through,
For there's always a tomorrow
And a chance to start anew.

— Author Unknown

Therefore, to him who knows to do good and does not do it, to him it is sin (James 4:17).

2. BE WILLING FOR CHANGE TO OCCUR

Be willing to "be made willing." Stubborn wills need to be broken. There is much value in "broken things." Someone has written the following thoughts:

It is on crushed grain that man is fed; it is by bruised plants that he is restored to health. It was by broken pitchers that Gideon triumphed; it was from a wasted barrel and empty cruse that the prophet was sustained; it was on boards and broken pieces of the ship that Paul and his companions were saved. It was amid the fragments of broken humanity that the promise of the higher life was given.

It is essential that personal willingness, desire and needs be offered to God. A deep-seated desire to change will be acknowledged by the Lord. He will then work in our lives to transform us.

> . . . for it is God who works in you both
> to will and to do for His good pleasure
> (Philippians 2:13).

This doesn't happen overnight. All of us hold back on God in some ways. It is difficult to face up, and give in. A willing, yielded spirit will break chains that bind us. God says He will be near those "who have a broken heart, and saves such as have a contrite spirit" (Psalm 34:18).

3. DETERMINE TO CHANGE. MAKE A DEFINITE COMMITMENT

Without commitment it is useless to expect change. Single minded attention is needed. "A double minded man is unstable in all his ways" (James 1:8).

The reason Abraham's faith did not waver when God asked him to offer up his only son was because of his commitment to God. Daniel refused to cease praying, because he was determined to honor God.

Why was Joseph enabled to withstand the temptation of going to bed with Potiphar's wife? Because of his single-minded determination and commitment to obey God.

Determination alone will not bring about change, but when this attribute is coupled with commitment, renewal and transformation will take place.

4. ASK GOD FOR WISDOM AND DIRECTION

Only God can supply the necessary armor to shield us against the enemy's attacks. It is not easy to change. It is more like being on a battlefield. A daily battle takes place between the flesh and the spirit.

What does it mean to ask for wisdom? In simple terms . . . Pray! God's word is specific in its direction: "If any of you lacks wisdom, let him ask of God, who gives to all liberally and without reproach, and it will be given to him (James 1:5).

Are you currently fighting battles in the flesh? Do you feel you are getting nowhere even though you've determined to live differently? What is the answer? Perhaps we are going about transformation in the wrong way. James 4:1-3 sparks understanding:

> Where do wars and fights come from among you? Do
> they not come from your desires for pleasure that war in
> your members? You lust and do not have . . . Yet you do
> not have because you do not ask. You ask and do not
> receive, because you ask amiss, that you may spend it
> on your pleasures.

There are two reasons why we do not receive: We do not ask, or
we ask for the wrong motives.

Why do we want to change? Is it because we want to please God
or others around us? Is it because others will praise, admire and com-
pliment us more? Do we want to change so we will be more popular,
happier or even more peaceful? It is true that we will experience more
peace and happiness, yet hidden motives may lie beneath the surface
which we do not recognize.

5. TOTALLY DEPEND UPON GOD

> Trust in the Lord with all your heart, and lean not unto
> your own understanding, in all your ways acknowledge
> Him and He will direct your paths (Proverbs 3:5,6).

> Trust in the Lord and do good, and He shall bring it to
> pass (Psalm 37:5).

The principle of total dependence on God comes with maturity
and experience. Trust in the Lord's leading and guidance at all times.
Lest this seem too simplistic, try counting all the faith-building verses
in the Bible. They are there for a reason. God tells us that without faith
it is impossible to please Him (Hebrews 11:6).

Where there is a trusting heart, God's steady hand will lead.

> Trust Him when dark doubts assail thee,
> Trust Him when thy strength is small,
> Trust Him when to simply trust Him,
> Seems the hardest thing of all.

> — Author Unknown

6. REMEMBER GOD DOES THE CHANGING

This point cannot be emphasized enough. The idea that you and
I bring about our own improvement is erroneous. Should we begin to
be proud of our accomplishments and boast of how well we are doing,
Satan will ensnare us.

Colossians 1:29 states:

> To this end I also labor, striving
> according to His working which works
> in me mightily.

Paul stated earlier that his goal was "that we may present every man perfect in Christ Jesus" (verse 28). This concept is expressed even more fully in Psalm 138:8: "He will perfect that which concerns me."

Will God truly perfect (complete) that which concerns me? He said He would. Do we believe Him?

Our trouble is that we try to pull ourselves up by our own bootstraps. We are forever "doing our own thing." What happens? We fall on our faces time and again. Oh, how foolish we are not to allow Jesus, our Lord, to perfect the changes which need to be made. He makes marvelous changes when we allow Him to do so.

C. S. Lewis wrote:

> Inviting Christ into our lives is like inviting a decorator
> into our homes to do a few minor changes; only to find
> that he has set about to remodel the whole house. He
> will make magnificent changes if we allow Him to. We
> try to build high rise hovels of our design. Babel has
> been tried before.

7. TAKE THE INITIAL STEP

In other words, set goals and begin taking positive steps to change any attitudes or actions which the Holy Spirit suggests to us through His Word.

His written living Word is where we must begin. God's Word convicts us of troubled areas in our lives.

When God, through the power of the holy Spirit, has helped us overcome one weakness of the flesh, He will begin to break down other barriers which have hindered us. Too often we have held back from Him, clutching our treasured practices to ourselves.

So where do we begin? We begin on our knees, asking the Father's wisdom and blessings on our new goals and purposes. Renewal doesn't begin "somewhere out there." It begins within.

> Our outward man is decaying, yet the
> inward man is being renewed day by
> day (2 Corinthians 4:16).

While our hair turns gray, our skin gets wrinkled and our shoulders become bent, we can become even more beautiful in our spirits.

8. CONFESS AND REPENT

After we have fallen on our knees in complete surrender to the perfect will of God, it is essential that we confess our sins and repent of them:

> If we confess our sins, He is faithful and just to forgive
> us our sins and to cleanse us from all unrighteousness
> (1 John 1:9).

Paul, speaking before King Agrippa, told how he had declared to both Jews and Gentiles "that they should repent, turn to God, and do works befitting repentance" (Acts 26:20).

We recognize our hopeless condition with bowed heads and "broken, contrite spirits." The Lord will then open the floodgates of heaven, calling us out of whatever personal darkness we are experiencing. All of us have had experiences which have left us humiliated and broken. The Hebrew word for "contrite" means "crushed, ground to powder."

A beautiful outpouring of brokenness is uttered by David in Psalm 51:17: "The sacrifices of God are a broken spirit, a broken and contrite heart, O God, You will not despise!"

On the contrary, our broken spirits (the shattering of pride and vanity) makes the Lord rejoice. The Lord truly hears and heeds our honest longings. "But on this one will I look: On Him who is poor and of a contrite spirit, And who trembles at My word" (Isaiah 66:2).

9. BELIEVE

Do we essentially believe we can be changed? In Mark 9:23, Jesus said: "If you can believe, all things are possible to him who believes."

Paul said in Philippians 4:13: "I can do all things through Christ who strengthens me."

We are "can do" people! By the strength and power which is our heritage from the Lord, we can do anything! His free gift of grace and power will be our strong platform from which we need never topple off again. The Bible does not tell us to "try harder." The Bible tells us to "believe harder." In Christ Jesus we find a constant source of strength and power.

10. CLAIM GOD'S PROMISES

Before we "launch out into the deep" we need to claim God's precious promises. They will be our own particular treasures; our own secret, vital answers for our specific needs.

For each specified personal need we can find many precious and cherished Scriptures. I have found many! I would like to think that you, too, are finding and claiming definite and specific verses which reach you personally — verses which reach down into your inner being and call you into obedience.

Oh, what power and hope we receive when we claim and believe God's personal promises to us. As a result, it seems natural to believe we *can* obey. As Isaiah 66:2 states, we need to "tremble at My word."

The Israelites were promised they would inherit the promised land of Canaan. All they were asked to do was "possess your possessions (Deuteronomy 1:8). God's promises are ours to claim, but it takes faith to appropriate them.

> Now to Him who is able to do exceedingly
> abundantly above all we ask or think, according
> to the power that works in us (Ephesians 3:20).

Step out with faith and not by sight. Make God's inspired Scriptures your very own. They are yours by possession!

One helpful thing you might want to do is to make a list of those areas in your life where you see changes are needed. I have made my list, perhaps you might want to so the same:

AREAS IN MY LIFE WHERE I WOULD LIKE THE LORD TO CHANGE ME

MY THOUGHTS

Whenever a negative, bad thought enters my mind, I will make an earnest attempt to replace it with a positive, wholesome thought. I will try to recall such passages as "...bringing every thought into captivity to the obedience of Christ" (2 Corinthians 10:5).

Also I must never forget Philippians 4:8:

> Finally, brethren, whatever things are true, whatever
> things are noble, whatever things are just, whatever
> things are pure, whatever things are lovely, whatever
> things are of good report, if there is any virtue and if
> there is anything praiseworthy — meditate on these
> things.

Lord,
Create in me a
clean heart,
And renew in me a
right spirit
(Psalm 51:20).
In Jesus' Name, Amen.

MY DEVOTIONAL LIFE

Be diligent to present yourself approved to God, a worker who does not need to be ashamed, rightly dividing the word of truth (2 Timothy 2:15).

I will try to set aside a given time and place to study and pray. I will try to prioritize my life so that first place is given to God. "Seek first the kingdom" will become a reality in my life when I value my "quiet time" above everything else. If something comes up to interfere with this time, I will try to study later in the day, but I will meditate on His Word and continue "instant in prayer" all through the day.

Lord, let the
highest
priority
Of my day . . .
Be the quiet hour
spent with
Thee.
In Jesus' Name, Amen.

MY RELATIONSHIP WITH MY HUSBAND

". . . the wife see that she respects her husband" (Ephesians 5:33).

I will cherish every precious moment with my husband. I will try to put other things aside when he is near. I will listen and respond to him in a way that will please him. I will give him first place in my heart, next to Christ. When he asks me to go somewhere or do something with him, I will try to do this.

If he is working at the table, I will try to bring my work where he is. If he is working in the yard, I will join him. I will try to show an interest in whatever he is interested. I will encourage "Bible talks" with him, as well as "Bible walks."

I will build him up, support, encourage and comfort him. I will try to make him the happiest man in the world.

Nor was man created for the woman; but the woman for the man (1 Corinthians 11:9).

> Lord, help me live
>   in complete love
>   and devotion
> To my husband,
>   giving you the
>   praise,
> For giving him to me.
>   In Jesus' Name, Amen.

MY RELATIONSHIP WITH OUR CHILDREN AND GRANDCHILDREN

I will stand by to help our wonderful family at any time. I will encourage them spiritually and pray for them daily. I will listen with the heart; looking them in the eye. I will put my work aside whenever possible. Nothing on earth is as important as our family.

I will praise my children and never undermine their esteem. I will pray for their mates and future mates. I will try to be an example to them, especially in my faith. I will try to be happy around them and show my joy in Jesus.

I will try to write them often. My prayer is that I will never do anything to make them ashamed of their mother and grandmother.

Deuteronomy 6 and John 17 are chapters I will always try to remember in my relationship with our family.

> Lord, help me to look
>   around at our
>   children
>   and grandchildren,
> And realize of all life's
>   blessings,
> Our family is the best.
> In Jesus' Name, Amen.

MY READING HABITS

I will try to fill my mind with the good, the wholesome and the uplifting. I will try to read often, especially the Word. I will attempt to strengthen my mind and increase my knowledge, so that I will be a good student, teacher and writer for the Lord.

Anthony Trollope stated:

> Book love, my friends is your pass to the greatest, the purest, and the most perfect pleasure that God has prepared for His creatures. It lasts when all other pleasures fade. It will support you when all other recreations are gone. It will last until your death. It will make your hours pleasant to you as long as you live.

> Lord, since reading is so
> Important in my life,
> Help me to read only
> What is
> true,
> honest,
> right,
> pure,
> lovely,
> excellent,
> praiseworthy.
> In Jesus' Name, Amen.

MY EATING HABITS

> Or do you not know that your body is the temple of the Holy Spirit who is in you, whom you have from God, and you are not your own? For you were bought with a price; therefore glorify God in your body and in your spirit, which are God's (1 Corinthians 6:19 and 20).

> Lord, help me to be
> truly positive
> about
> eating and drinking
> only strength
> building food and drink.
> In Jesus' Name, Amen.

MY EXERCISES

For bodily exercise profits a little, but godliness is profitable for all things, having promise of the life that now is and of that which is to come (1 Timothy 4:8).

I will try to keep my body active as long as I can, in order to be strong for my Lord. I will especially try to walk in the mornings or evenings.

Lord,
You know how I hate
    to exercise.
Please help me plan a
    healthy, disciplined
    program of exercise
Which will strengthen
    my physical body
        for
    greater service
        to You.
In Jesus' Name, Amen.

MY WORK

And whatever you do in word or deed, do all in the name of the Lord Jesus, giving thanks to God the Father through Him (Colossians 3:17).

I will try to be more organized in my work — putting first things first. I will try to find joy in the accomplishment of my hands, remembering that my work as a homemaker, mother and wife is the most important in the world. As a writer and teacher, my work is rewarding, but building a home is my primary desire. I will find satisfaction in serving in these areas.

I will try not to feel frustrated when something I had planned to do is left undone. I will find joy with what has been accomplished.

> Lord,
> Help me plan a
> Sensible schedule
> Of work.
> Balancing
> Housework
> Cooking
> Studying
> Writing
> Teaching
> Mothering and
> Grandmothering.
> In Jesus' Name, Amen.

SOUL WINNING

> And on some have compassion, making a distinction; but others save with fear, pulling them out of the fire, hating even the garment defiled by the flesh (Jude 22,23).

Every person I meet is a living soul who will spend eternity somewhere. My daily prayer is that I will take advantage of the opportunities made available to teach the lost.

I also pray that the Lord will take away all fear and anxiety so that I will be willing to be involved in the lives of others. I need to know that He is with me and will help me to say and do the right things.

> Lord,
> Help me to "think"
> souls
> And lead others
> to Thee.
> In Jesus' Name, Amen.

MY DAILY ATTITUDES

> Your attitude should be the same as that of Christ Jesus: (Philippians 2:5) NIV

Change for the better begins with my daily attitudes. When I look at Jesus, beholding Him as in a mirror, I know that I shall be transformed into His image, from glory to glory, as by the Spirit of the Lord (2 Corinthians 3:18). When I begin practicing *His* attitudes, my disposition will be that of a radiant, happy, thankful Christian woman.

Lord,
Please don't let me
Criticize
Or judge
Anyone . . .
Especially
In my thoughts . . .
Much less the
Spoken word.
In Jesus' Name, Amen.

I can see God's perfect work in my life when I begin to grow and change. Transformation will come about only when I yield myself and all my habits, good or bad, to Him. Through prayer and obedience I can be made into God's beautiful woman.

Faithfully Yours,
Judy

THINK ON THESE THINGS

1. How do we obtain the power to change?

2. How can pinpointing specific needs help us in changing?

3. (True or false?) Change takes place swiftly and easily.

4. Can we expect change without commitment? Why not?

5. What does it mean to ask for wisdom?

6. Discuss reasons why change is a mark of maturity.

7. How does total dependence on God come about?

8. In what way does the reading of Psalm 138:8 encourage us?

9. How do we find out what changes need to be made?

10. What does the Hebrew word for "contrite" mean?

11. (True or false?) We are perfectly capable of making changes in our own lives, by ourselves.

12. Change for the better begins with ________ ________ .

13. Memorize and meditate upon Ephesians 3:20.

14. Make a list of the areas in your life where you wish to change.

Chapter Nine

God's Gift of Self-Control

It must have been cold that night. Peter huddled in his cloak around the warm fire which had been kindled in the court of the high priest's house.

He had followed Jesus from afar, and now he sat among the Roman soldiers and servants of the high priest who were warming their hands as well.

As the fire flamed higher and brighter, one of the servant girls looked intently at Peter. She thought she recognized him as being one of Jesus' followers. Aloud, she said, "This man was also with Him."

Peter, stepping backward, cried vehemently, "Woman, I do not know Him." He must have gathered his cloak closer, perhaps to hide his appearance. Another servant saw him and said, "This fellow also was with Jesus of Nazareth."

But again he denied with an oath, "I do not know the man!"

After awhile those who stood by came to him and said, "Surely you also are one of them, because your speech betrays you." Others, standing near, nodded in agreement with the man's statement.

Peter denied the third time. "Man, I do not know what you are saying!"

> And immediately, while he was still speaking, the rooster crowed. And the Lord turned and looked at Peter (Luke 22:60,61).

Then Peter "remembered the word of the Lord" (Luke 22:61). Peter remembered! Oh he remembered! Jesus had told him that before the night was over, he would deny Him.

When it hit his soul what he had done, he went out and wept bitterly and uncontrollably.

Uncontrollably! Peter had been out of control a long time. Perhaps he was remembering the events of the evening. At the very table where Jesus sat, he had asked, among the others, who would be the greatest in His kingdom.

And the Lord said, "Simon, Simon! Indeed, Satan has asked for you, that he may sift you as wheat. But I have prayed for you, that your faith should not fail; and when you have returned to Me, strengthen your brethren" (Luke 22:31,32).

> But he said to Him, "Lord, I am ready to go with You,
> both to prison and to death." Then He said, "I tell you,
> Peter, the rooster will not crow this day before you will
> deny three times that you know me" (Luke 22:34).

It had happened as His Lord had said. Other times Peter had been out of control. Jesus had gone to the garden that night with his closest and dearest friends. He said to His disciples, "Sit here while I pray."

Jesus had fallen on the ground, praying that if it were possible, the cup that He was about to bear might be taken from Him.

> "Nevertheless, not what I will, but what
> You will" (Mark 14:36).

He turned to find his apostles sleeping; and said to Peter: "Simon, are you sleeping? Could you not watch one hour?" (v.37).

> "Watch and pray, lest you enter into
> temptation. The spirit truly is ready,
> but the flesh is weak" (Mark 14:38).

How true! Three times Jesus went aside to pray, and three times He came and found them asleep. Yes, Peter was out of control.

We could relate other stories about Peter. All along he had been in the school room of Christ, and yet he had not learned to control himself. What was his nature?

He was impetuous, impulsive, stubborn — often headstrong and angry. He spoke without thinking — acted without regard for the consequences.

I'm sure it took the death and resurrection of our Lord before Peter was totally converted, totally transformed, and became the Peter of the book of Acts who presented the sermon on the day of Pentecost.

After experiencing the love and forgiveness of Christ, Peter could write these words in his first book:

> Therefore humble yourselves under the mighty hand of
> God, that he may exalt you in due time, casting all your
> care upon Him, for He cares for you (1 Peter 5:6,7).

SELF-CONTROL DEFINED

It was interesting for me to research the word "self-control" in the Webster's dictionary and find that it was defined as "control of self." "That's a very limited meaning," I thought, so I also researched the word in a Bible dictionary. Here we find "self-control" defined as "the controlling power of the will under the power of God."

When the Bible speaks of self-control, it uses a term which literally means "inwardly strong." We might define it as "inner strength."

As we think of self-control, we sometimes think of "self at the controls." None of us find it easy to be controlled. We do not like for anyone to tell us what to do. We like to do it on our own.

We know that self-control involves restraint from many of our impulses and desires.

SELF CONTROL AS A FRUIT OF THE SPIRIT

> But the fruit of the Spirit is love, joy, peace, long-suffering, kindness, goodness, faithfulness, gentleness, self-control. Against such there is no law (Galatians 5:22,23).

The harvest of the Spirit will produce these attributes in the human spirit. Self-control is the last named fruit of the Spirit, but that does make not make it any less important. All the fruits of the spirit are centered in love, the first named fruit. Self-control is the perfection of love.

We cannot be controlled by the Spirit unless we manifest love. Unless we love our Lord we can never conquer the sinful flesh. The flesh and the spirit are always going to be at war. We have great help from the Spirit. When we are spirit controlled, we have great mastery over our desires and impulses:

> You, however, are controlled not by your sinful nature but by the Spirit, if the Spirit of God lives in you. And if anyone does not have the Spirit of Christ, he does not belong to Christ (Romans 8:9). NIV

When you are filled with the Spirit you will be self-controlled:

> I say then: Walk in the Spirit, and you
> shall not fulfill the lust of the flesh
> (Galatians 5:16).

We have an *old* self which constantly springs up to control our *new* self. When the Spirit is in control, He rules our lives. He empowers us to be controlled regardless of how we feel.

Many times we are controlled by feelings. We feel certain ways, so we act upon it. "If it feels good, do it," is the philosophy of the world. If we don't feel like doing something, we don't do it. If we feel like saying something, we say it.

Paul had this constant struggle with the flesh. Even he did not understand the struggles which beset him:

> For the good that I will to do, I do not
> do; but the evil I will not to do, that I
> practice . . . O wretched man that I am!
> Who will deliver me from this body of
> death? I thank God — through Jesus
> Christ our Lord! So then, with the mind
> I myself serve the law of God, but with
> the flesh the law of sin (Roman 7:19 and
> 24, 25).

TROUBLE AREAS

Are we like Paul, in that we feel the things we want to do, we do not; or the things we shouldn't do, we find ourselves doing?

The various powers bestowed upon us are capable of being abused. Lack of control may be found in the following areas:

Losing temper
Bad thoughts
Lying
Overeating or undereating
Neglecting Bible study and prayer
Worry
Promiscuity
Emotional outbursts

There is one area where many of us have problems — the use of the tongue:

> But no man can tame the tongue. It is
> an unruly evil, full of deadly poison
> (James 3:8).

Yes, it is true no *man* can tame the tongue, but One can tame our tongue. Christ can control our tongues as we allow Him to.

We can really inject permanent damage on our children when we affect them negatively with our tongues.

We can ruin an honest person's reputation by slandering them or by gossiping about them. We can quench a young person's potential for good by telling them that they will never amount to anything.

Careless and bitter words are destructive. We can destroy people with our words. Jesus said:

> For out of the abundance of the heart the mouth speaks.
> A good man out of the good treasure of his heart brings
> forth good things, and an evil man out of the evil trea-
> sure brings forth evil things. But I say to you that for
> every idle word men may speak, they will give account
> of it in the day of judgment. For by your words you will
> be justified, and by your words you will be condemned
> (Matthew 12:34-37).

As we speak, the heart is revealed. The lips expose what is in our hearts. The person who will attack another person with words is telling more about himself than the person he condemns.

When God reigns in our hearts, we will speak words of encouragement, kindness and praise. Also, we should never let other people's words control our own. It matters not what others may say, but it does matter how we respond.

SELF-CONTROL, ONE OF THE CHRISTIAN GRACES

> But also for this very reason, giving all diligence, add to
> your faith virtue, to virtue, knowledge, to knowledge
> self-control, to self-control perseverance, to perse-
> verance godliness, to godliness brotherly kindness, and
> to brotherly kindness love. (2 Peter 1:5-7).

Self-control follows "knowledge," suggesting that it is a learned response, not an automatic one. Self-control is the possession of the emotionally mature. Children are not born self-controlled — they have to be carefully taught to be. All of us must develop control. It is a trait all Christians must cultivate.

We grow "in the grace and knowledge" of self-control as we learn to follow in the footsteps of Jesus.   To be self-controlled is to be balanced. Balance and poise were surely beautiful attributes Jesus possessed. Once we get to "know" Christ and take His characteristics into our own lives, we know that self-control will follow.

SELF-CONTROL AND OUR PERSONALITIES

Our personalities tell others about who we are and to Whom we belong. One important factor in becoming a Christian is that we soon learn that Jesus Christ can change our personalities. God's kindness and goodness is meant to lead us to a change of heart:

> Are you unmindful or actually ignorant
> (of the fact) that God's kindness is in-
> tended to lead you to repent — to
> change your mind and inner man to
> accept God's will?   (Romans 2:4—
> Amplified Version).

We need to keep relearning and practicing the above Scripture throughout the remainder of our lives. Another thing we need to remember is that Christ takes control of our lives to the degree we allow Him. "For the love of Christ constrains us: (2 Corinthians 5:14).

What a difference it makes in a woman's life whether she is self-controlled or Christ-controlled! People need to *see* the difference. Christ should make a dynamic, noticeable difference. I believe one of the reasons others come to know and believe Christ, is because of the changes they see in our own lives.

All the uncontrolled power in us can be controlled by the very life of Christ:

> I have been crucified with Christ; it is
> no longer I who live, but Christ lives in
> me; and the life which I now live in the
> flesh I live by faith in the Son of God
> who loved me and gave Himself for me.
> (Galatians 2:20).

We cannot cope with life by ourselves. We need Someone in whom we can have confidence; Someone we can fully trust. This beautiful peace, trust and confidence gives us the ability to live and act under God's will.

When we think about it, no good thing exists within ourselves, but in Christ "we can do all things." We have a power to do evil and a power to do good. The evil power within destroys people, but Christ's power always builds and never tears down.

Let us face the fact that we women have a strong influential hold over those in our lives. We mark lives! The marks we leave will be determined by control or lack of it.

Troubled areas exist in all our lives, but there are also beautiful areas of control. These will wield a powerful influence in the lives of our families and loved ones — not because of who we are but because of Who He is.

Think of your own troubled areas. Make a list. Ask for God's help. If they come to mind, we probably lack self-control in these areas.

We may not see the good in our blunders and mistakes, but God can "make all things work together for good." As we come to Him in faith and contrition, He will forgive us. We can go on trying to live better.

This is where faith enters in. "For we walk by faith, not by sight" (2 Corinthians 5:7). Too many of us want to *see* what Christ is doing. If we will only be patient, He will show us His plan for us. Learning to wait is difficult, but through our waiting experiences we learn self-control.

CONTROL OF OUR DISPOSITIONS

One of the ways people can tell we are Christ-controlled is in our dispositions. A woman's disposition is an outward sign of what she is on the inside.

> ... but let it be the hidden person of the
> heart, with the incorruptible ornament
> of a gentle and quiet spirit, which is
> very precious in the sight of God (1
> Peter 3:4).

Christ was God-controlled, and we must remember that He was in all points tempted as we are:

> For we do not have a High Priest who
> cannot sympathize with our weak-
> nesses, but was in all points tempted as
> we are, yet without sin (Hebrews 4:15).

We must form the habit of choosing to let Christ act through us. Sometimes our actions speak louder than words. We must choose whether we will be "ourselves" or let Him be "Himself."

At all times, under all circumstances, we should be controlled through the power of Christ. We do not have a right to excuse our irritability, nagging, and unbridled tongues on the basis that "women are just like that."

Younger women often use Premenstrual Syndrome as an excuse for irritability. This may be the reason we are not feeling our best, but if we are Christ-controlled, we need not be cross and impatient.

Middle-aged women excuse their actions on the basis that they may be going through the change of life. I don't know what excuse older women can give except "old age." Older women should be the sweetest, kindest, gentlest, most winsome people in the world. After years of living with Christ, His nature should be deeply ingrained within.

A woman's disposition tells others who is in control of her life. If Christ is predominant, it will come out in our dispositions.

CONTROL IN OUR MIND AND THOUGHTS

The Christian woman's *mind* must continually be renewed. We must frequently remind ourselves that we are not to be "conformed to this world, but we are to be transformed by the renewing of our minds: (Romans 12:2). "For as he thinks in his heart, so is he" (Proverbs 23:7) should be indelibly stamped on our minds.

> Therefore, since Christ suffered for us
> in the flesh, arm yourselves also with
> the same mind (1 Peter 4:1).

Christ controls our total personalities as we allow Him to work with our minds. One of the disciplines of the godly woman is the discipline of her mind:

> Let this mind be in you which was also
> in Christ Jesus (Philippians 2:5).

We need to remember that Christ works with our minds through our habits. Habits are not formed overnight — it requires time to form new habits. Christ needs to work with our habits, and we need to give Him time to do so.

Forming new habits of control does not always mean an act of our wills. We are transformed by *holding Christ in our minds*. We "imagine" ourselves being like Christ until we become more like Him. A mental picture (image) of what we should like to be, or, should I say *Who* we should be like, will keep us on target as we strive to reach our goals:

> But we all, with unveiled face, behold-
> ing as in a mirror the glory of the Lord,
> are being transformed into the same
> image from glory to glory, just as by the
> Spirit of the Lord (2 Corinthians 3:18).

Imagination means "holding an image in our minds." We tend to exhibit in our lives the kind of images we hold in our minds.

It is helpful for us to remember that the mind is like a battlefield. A description of the battlefield is given in Ephesians 6:10-13. This conflict is more real than most of us realize.

We should not be ignorant of Satan's control of our minds. Paul wrote in 2 Corinthians 2:9 and 11:

> For to this end I also write that I might
> put you to the test, whether you are
> obedient in all things . . . lest Satan
> should take advantage of us: for we are
> not ignorant of his devices.

Christ desires that we be "obedient in all things." How can we capture our minds "to the obedience of Christ?"

> For the weapons of our warfare are not
> carnal but mighty in God for pulling
> down strongholds, casting down argu-
> ments and every high thing that exalts
> itself against the knowledge of God,
> bringing every thought into captivity to
> the obedience of Christ (2 Corinthians
> 10:4 and 5).

One of the best ways to bring "every thought into captivity" is to memorize Scripture. Nothing will help us "put on the whole armor of God" as much as committing passages of Scripture to mind. We read in Job 22:21-23:

> Now acquaint yourself with Him, and be at peace;
> Therefore good will come to you.
> Receive, please, instruction from His mouth,
> And lay up His words in your heart.
> If you return to the Almighty, you will be built up;
> You will remove iniquity from your tents.

SEVERAL REASONS WHY WE LOSE CONTROL

Ingratitude

> But know this, that in the last days
> perilous times will come: For men will
> be lovers of themselves, lovers of
> money, boasters, proud, blasphemers,
> disobedient to parents, unthankful, un-
> holy . . .   (2 Timothy 3:1,2).

One of the most powerful lessons we can teach our children is to be grateful. Teach them to thank God and people, for no one enjoys the company of an ungrateful person.

Shakespeare aptly expressed it when he wrote:

> Blow, blow, thou winter wind.
> Thou art not so unkind
>   As man's ingratitude.

The child who is taught to be grateful and thankful is a blessed child. We, too, must learn to be grateful for it will teach us to have a "gentle, quiet spirit" as will nothing else. When we spend our days in grateful appreciation for all God and others do for us, we will cease complaining. We see things from a new perspective, (these are gifts!) and our dispositions will be changed.

We find it easy to be controlled in the morning when we are fresh and energetic, but the evenings become a different story. What is the problem?

Fatigue

Fatigue is certainly a problem with most of us. Usually the time when we are tired and worn out is the period we experience the greatest loss of self-control. As the day goes on and our nerves grow weary, our control weakens.

Small children, teenagers, or stress at work may cause our nerves to snap. Problems and obstacles seem to mount up, and we can handle them best in the morning; but at night everything seems more difficult to endure.

Almost always after a sleepless night, or two or three, we find it almost impossible to be under control. At times like this, it is difficult to muster up any kind of control.

Another time when we have problems with control is during:

Pain and Suffering

Disappointments, worries, hurts, uncertainties can be roots of irritability. Tempers can easily flare in times of pain. We know headaches can make us feel cross. Just to be in pain, to hurt, to be sick — all these things make us feel weak and out of control. To have a backache or the cramps makes us feel restless and uneasy. We blame these situations rather than taking them as warning signals.

Temper or crossness does not come on without some sort of warning. Just as a thunder storm does not come without some kind of warning, neither do our times of being "out of sorts." Just before a thunderstorm, we observe black clouds, oppressive heat, and sudden stillness. So the storms of temper and anger give warning of their coming.

If we can learn to recognize the warning signals such as ingratitude, pain and suffering, disappointments, worry and uncertainties, we will be able to keep the storms of uncontrollability from hitting so hard.

Time Pressures

Another frequent sign of oncoming temper is pressure from lack of time. This is an oft-felt feeling that we'll never get anything done and too many demands are being made upon us. Dr. James Dobson calls this "time pressures."

We know that too many pressures and demands causes stress. Stress, as it builds up, tends to cause us to lose control. A woman may feel that no matter how much she tries, she'll never catch up — also the feeling that no one ever notices anyway, so what difference does it make?

A feeling of helplessness leads to depression and discouragement. In such circumstances, a woman can easily feel sorry for herself, and this causes her to lash out at her family. If only her husband, daughter or son would applaud her work.

Dr. James Dobson also says that everyone needs at least one person to be in his or her "Amen corner" . . . a supporter to build up. A husband who understands his wife's restlessness is caused by being with preschool children all day, and tells her so, is a wise man.

If we do not have anyone to support and encourage us, let us not use that as an excuse for "losing it." God encourages and builds us up daily as we hear Him speak to us through His Word.

Indecision

Another warning signal is when we find it hard to make up our mind. Decisions! They are always with us, so constant, we wish someone else would make them for us.

Sometimes little decisions are harder to make than big ones. They prey on our minds, and we lose sleep, causing us to go in a vicious circle. Confusion often results in lack of control.

What happens? We find ourselves in a bad mood. Our moods should never be the criteria of decision making. Judgments are marred many times by indecisiveness.

Many times what is needed most is *rest.* Also getting away for a little while will work marvels. Get away from the children, get away from the immediate problem, delay making decisions until our minds are more settled.

Bible reading and prayer will rest and restore us more than any one activity. Drinking from the fountain of His Word will quench our thirsty spirits and revitalize us.

SELF-CONTROL REQUIRES SELF-DISCIPLINE

Discipline is not easy, yet discipline is the price we pay for freedom:

> He who is slow to anger is better than
> the mighty, And he who rules his spirit
> than he who takes a city (Proverbs
> 16:32).

Discipline is a liberator. It will set us free from the tyranny of laziness, slothfulness and other harmful habits. It will also restore our freedom of choice.

Tensions have a way of diminishing in proportion to discipline and control. Both the spirit and body have to be disciplined. When the will is firm and the body is strong, there is almost nothing a person cannot do. There are tremendous awards in discipline.

We must discipline ourselves to the point where we "die to self." Self is the greatest enemy of control. Selfishness restrains, confines and turns us inward. Paul said "I die daily" (1 Corinthians 15:31).

We die to self when our fleshly life is replaced by the spiritual life. Someone has said:

> Just as a tree must drop its old leaves
> before the sap of the new life rises
> within it in the spring, so the old
> desires, ideals, and inclinations must
> disappear before the rising new life of
> Christ.
> — Author Unknown

After a recent workshop conducted in a small Texas town, I received the following letter from one of the ladies who sat in my Sunday morning class:

> When I was going through the sleepless nights and Satan was causing my mind to run away with all sorts of imaginings and sleep would not come — I would get up and put a tape on and think of the words. Also books written by Christians were beneficial to the healing process.
>
> God has blessed me in so many ways — with "Roses along the thorny path." You see, Judy, for 47 years I had lived in a Rose Garden" and I did not know how to endure the thorns, but God has helped me to endure.

God will not always line our thorny paths with roses, but He will provide us a way to go through them. Sometimes the only way we can grow in self-control is to be tested to the point where we know only God can give us the power to endure. Steadfast endurance brings about the peaceful fruit of disciplined control.

HOLD TO GOD'S UNCHANGING HAND

Once there was a talented puppeteer who was performing before a large audience. On a vast stage he manipulated a funny clown marionette.

The puppet almost seemed to come alive under the skilled hands of the puppeteer. The marionette danced to a sprightly tune to the audience's delight.

All of a sudden, the marionette caught sight of the puppeteer's actions. Frowning, he decided he wanted to be free. He stopped, deliberated, then snapped the strings on one arm.

As this happened, he became lop-sighted and disjointed. One arm lay dangling, under the control of no one. The other arm remained under his master's manipulations, but no longer could he dance with grace and beauty. Yet he was determined that he would not have the puppeteer controlling him.

Finally a very pathetic and forlorn little figure dangled by one arm. Undaunted, he snapped the controls of the remaining string, falling in a lifeless heap on the stage.

There may be times in our lives, when we feel exactly like this marionette. We wish to pull free from what we consider to be the restraining hand of God. God does not manipulate His people — He upholds, directs, guides and corrects us with His loving hands:

> Fear not, for I am with you;
> Be not dismayed, for I am your God.
> I will strengthen you,
> Yes, I will help you,
> I will uphold you with My *righteous right hand.*
>
> (Isaiah 41:10) — Emphasis Added.

I remember very clearly the time our four-year-old grandson, Matthew, was visiting in our home. My husband plays the piano "by ear" very beautifully.

One day, Matthew asked Grandpa if he could play the piano with him. Grandpa took Matthew on his knee and placed his hands on the key.

"Can we play 'Mary had a little lamb,' Grandpa?" asked Matthew. "Yes, we can, Matthew," said Grandpa. "Place your forefinger under my hand, and let me direct your fingers. We will play 'Mary had a little lamb' together."

Matthew did not want to do this. He did not want Grandpa's hand on his — he pushed it away, and started playing on his own.

There was no tune, no melody — he had lost it all. Grandpa whispered gently to Matthew:

"Matthew, you can play a beautiful song if you will only let your finger lie under Grandpa's hand."

When Matthew learned to surrender his hand to his Grandpa's, the two of them began to play a wonderful song together.

Jesus tells us we must lose ourselves for His sake (Luke 9:24). We must place our lives totally under His care. His hand on ours will cause our lives to be beautifully controlled.

I tend to splinter all apart
With fractured mind, divided heart,
Oh, integrate my wandering maze
To one highway of love and praise.
Keep gathering back my heart to You
Keep centering all I am to do.
Help me drop the clutter from my soul
Reorganized by Your control.
Then single, whole before Your throne,
I give myself to You alone.

— Author Unknown

Faithfully Yours,
Judy

THINK ON THESE THINGS

1. .Describe Peter's nature.

2. Share aloud passages from the writings of Peter which illustrate how Christ had altered his life.

3. The dictionary defines self-control as ______________ ____ ________ .

4. How does the Bible dictionary define self-control?

5. In what areas do you lack control?

6. As we speak to one another, the ______________ is revealed.

7. Self control is the possession of the ______________ ______________ .

8. True or false? Self-control involves restraint from many of our impulses and desires.

9. We cannot be controlled by the Spirit unless we manifest ________ .

10. Name one area where others can really tell whether or not we are self-controlled.

11. Christ comes in and takes control of our lives to the ________ we ________ _____ _____ .

12. What does imagination mean?

13. Name a good way to bring "every thought into captivity."

14. Memorize Proverbs 16:32 today, and share it with someone.

Chapter Ten

Seeking the Lost

INTRODUCTION:

Jesus, the Master Teacher, rarely used a three syllable word. He didn't talk down to His audience. He used words that they understood. His object lessons were about things common to their daily lives. He used comparisons between familiar facts and spiritual truths — "speaking to them by parables." In this lesson we will study three of His "short stories" and look for the applications in our daily lives.

THE LOST SHEEP
Matthew 18:12-14; Luke 15:3-7

A certain shepherd had one hundred sheep. Every day he counted them as they passed by. One day he counted 96, 97, 98, 99. One was missing!

This good shepherd loved his sheep, protected them from wild animals, doctored them when they were injured, carried those that were too tired or too young to walk and knew each one by name.

Did the shepherd say of the lost sheep, "Well, one out of a hundred isn't bad. Maybe it will show up. If it doesn't, and if I have time tomorrow, I will look for it?" NO! He left the ninety and nine and searched until he found his lost sheep. He lifted the frightened sheep upon his shoulder and hurried home, calling to his friends and neighbors saying: "Rejoice with me for I have found my sheep which was lost" (Luke 15:6).

For centuries artists have depicted *their conception* of this poignant scene of Jesus with a lamb on His shoulder. This art still is hanging in famous art galleries, in palaces and in "average" homes. It can be found on wall plaques, on calendars, in books and on that long ago and far away "Sunday School Card" that was used to teach beginners in Bible classes. Of course, no one knows what Jesus looked like, but there is no sweeter way to *imagine* how He looked than to think of Him with a lamb around His neck or in His arms — LOST, BUT FOUND!

LESSONS FOR CHRISTIANS:

1. Stay in the fold, near The Good Shepherd.
2. Watch for "straying" Christians. Help them find their way ... home.
3. Uplift the fallen, as Jesus lifted the sheep *up* to His shoulder.
4. Rejoice when the lost is found!

It isn't always the young who stray. Jesus does not call this lost sheep a *lamb*, a *baby sheep*, or a *young* sheep. From this we can draw the conclusion that "straying" or "getting lost" is not peculiar to one age group.

THE LOST COIN
Luke 15:8-10

There was a custom in Palestine for a woman to wear a head-dress bedecked with coins. These coins had more than a monetary value, they often were treasured heirlooms or part of a woman's dowry.

Jesus tells of a woman who had ten pieces of silver. She lost *one*. Did she say, "I have nine more, and though I am sorry, there is nothing to do but accept the fact that is is lost?" NO!

First, the woman freely admits she lost the coin. It was once in her possession and she "let it get away."

Second, she "turned on the light" in order to search for the lost coin. She swept every "nook and cranny."

Third, she didn't give up. Jesus said, "she sought diligently for it until she found it."

As the shepherd did, the woman called her friends to rejoice with her. She wanted to share the good news with her friends and neighbors.

Jesus was a master at using earthly stories to teach spiritual lessons. What are some lessons we may draw from this parable?

1. Freely admit our sins. "Confess therefore your sins one to another" (James 5:16). Exhaust every effort to right them, and every effort to find the lost.

2. "Turn on the light" of God's word in our lives, so that we may see into every nook and corner.

3. The coin was lost at home. How many husbands, wives, and children are "lost at home?" If this should be the case in our home then we must do as the woman in the parable did, we must "search diligently" for them until they are found.

When we find the lost we must make it safe. And then rejoice!

We will want to do as the woman and the shepherd did, we will want to share the "good news" (the gospel of Christ) with our friends and neighbors.

> Even so, I say unto you, there is joy in
> the presence of the angels of God over
> one sinner that repenteth (Luke 15:10).

THE LOST SON
Luke 15:11-32

Jesus had used the parable of an animal (sheep) and of an inanimate object (coin) and now He used MAN, His Creation who is a living soul that will live eternally somewhere. All three parables were designed to enlighten His disciples, including us today, concerning the urgency of seeking the lost and to share the good news with others. Jesus taught that *one* soul is more valuable than the whole world: "For what is a man profited, if he shall gain the whole world, and lose his own soul?" (Matthew 16:26 KJV). Imagine, if you can, the combined assets of the whole world: buildings, lands, minerals, gems, stocks and bonds, etc., all combined, are not worth the value of ONE soul!

"There was a man who had two sons," Jesus said. The younger son asked for his inheritance from his father. He wanted OUT. He wanted no part of "sticking at home" with his family. He wanted to make it on his own — go it alone! The father gave him his part and allowed him to go.

The son went into a far country and lived it up! Ah, the freedom of being away from the restrictions of a father and an older brother. This was living — money to spend and no one to dictate how to spend it. After all, this money was rightfully his; he didn't steal it, so why shouldn't he use it as he pleased?

Then a severe famine spread over that country — a depression. His money was all gone and his fair-weather friends left him. He had no job. But even if he had money, there was no food to buy. Finally, a citizen of that country gave him a job. But what a job! Taking care of swine. No Jew ever was associated with swine.

Surely, this was the depths of degradation. But no, this young man had one more downward step to go. He became so hungry he would gladly have eaten the food that the pigs were eating, but "no man gave unto him."

At last, he came to his senses and realized that the hired servants in his father's house had more than they could eat. And here he is perishing with hunger. The Bible says, "when he came to himself" he said:

> I will arise and go to my father, and will
> say unto him, Father, I have sinned . . . I
> am no more worthy to be called thy son:
> make me as one of thy hired servants
> (Luke 15:18,19).

This young man had evidently been taught to appreciate the values of home life, and when put to the test he did "not depart from them." The teachings of moral values, of love for home and family are most effective when shared by both father and mother. One wonders how much the memory of a godly mother played in the restoration of this son — causing him to "come to himself."

> My son, hear the instructions of thy father,
> and forsake not the law of thy mother (Proverbs 1:8).

The Holy Spirit says, "He arose, and came to his father" (verse 20). Could this father have been watching day by day for his son to return? The son must come back voluntarily, but the father eagerly awaits his return. One day while the son was still a long way off, his father saw him in the distance. His heart was filled with compassion and he RAN to meet his son. He threw his arms around him and kissed him.

Now the son confesses to his father, using the exact words that he said to himself back in the pig pen. This was not brought about because of his circumstances, but as genuine repentance and confession. It is true that he made good that promise to admit his sins and return to his father. What a powerful lesson that Jesus taught in these words easily understood. Powerful! *Full of power*. The father said to a servant:

1. Bring the best robe. A robe was a mark of distinction given to honored guests.
2. Bring a ring. A ring was a sign of authority. He had been restored to his place as a son of his father!
3. Bring sandals for his feet. Sandals were a luxury, worn only by *free* men. No slave wore sandals. This son was free of his old life style; he had been forgiven and was once again received as a SON.
4. Bring the fatted calf. A prize calf was always kept up and fattened to be used on special occasions or in case of a visit by a dignitary. Surely, this was a special occasion because a special one had come home. The happy father said: "This my son was dead, and is alive again; he was lost, and is found" (Luke 15:24). LOST, BUT FOUND!

LOST AND *NOT* FOUND

In all three parables the lost was found. There are many earthly things that we lose but we usually find them. If not found, we often can replace them — such as houses, lands, personal possessions, etc. There are, however, some things that we lose that are never found. For example:

TEMPER: A lost temper produces angry words that can never be taken back. The spoken word hangs over our head like a cloud. If words are spoken in anger because we"lost" our temper they often cause hurt and despair. Robert Fulghum, in his book, *All I Really Need to Know I Learned in Kindergarten* (Villard Books), said: "Sticks and stones may break our bones, but words will break our hearts."

How many hearts have been broken, how many homes have been broken, how many souls have been "lost but NOT found," because of angry words? All because of a *lost* temper!

OPPORTUNITIES: Lost opportunities! All too often *that particular* opportunity does not come again. We may, like Esau of old, seek it "diligently with tears" yet that opportunity is lost forever. But, as the shepherd and the woman in the other parables did, we should "search diligently" for other chances of service and be careful not to lose them. And as the father did we should watch day by day and then RUN to any door of opportunity that is opened for us. With knowledge and ability comes responsibility.

> To him therefore that knoweth to do good, and doeth it not, to him it is sin (James 4:17).

> We must work . . . while it is day: the night cometh, when no man can work (John 9:4).

INTEGRITY: In a world where men in high places of authority seemingly have no regard for moral ethics, and in a world where men are mad with power, it is easy to say "everybody does it." Some lose their integrity never to be restored!

Yet, everybody does not sacrifice principle for power. Many fine men and women choose righteousness over "recognition." True, they are in the minority and must sometimes feel alone, as did Elijah. He thought he was the only prophet of God left in all Israel. However, any minority with God becomes a majority.

VIRGINITY: Once lost, virginity can never be found — even God cannot restore it. He can and will, however, forgive when one repents of any sin. He will "blot-out" sins and "remember them no more" (Hebrews 8:12).

> If we confess our sins, he is faithful and righteous to forgive us our sins, and to cleanse us from all unrighteousness (1 John 1:9).

It is unlikely that a teenager will ever see inside this book. But, those using these lessons as a study guide may have the opportunity to teach girls *and* boys in a Bible class or at home the importance of avoiding the sin of fornication. It should be stressed, however, that they can be forgiven if guilty of this sin and urge them not to delay in repenting and asking God to forgive them.

Pressures and temptations are seemingly greater than ever before in the lives of teenagers. If young people are not taught to rightfully use the sex drive, they can easily find themselves yielding to the "everybody does it" mold. It is mid-Victorian to believe or teach a double standard for girls and boys. Usually we appeal to young ladies to "keep yourselves pure for your husbands." We *should* appeal to them: "keep yourselves pure for yourselves." Boys should be taught to respect girls and that *their* own body should be kept pure. Some of the last words spoken by the Apostle Paul were addressed to the young man Timothy:

> Let no man despise thy youth; but be thou an example to them (1 Timothy 4:12).

In 1 Timothy 5:22, Paul says to Timothy, "Keep thyself pure."

CONCLUSION

The shepherd with his lost sheep and the woman with her lost coin were in their own home environment when they lost and found their treasures.

We need not go out of our home environment to find souls who are lost in sin. There are some in our own neighborhood who have lost their purpose for living and need help to find their way. We need to "search diligently" for opportunities to help them.

The first two parables teach the urgency that Christians should feel toward helping restore lost souls, having faith that God will bless their efforts.

In the third parable the son went away from his home into a"far country." A far country can be different things to different people. It can be a state of mind. For example, one person may stay at home and yet his heart be in a "far country" — far from the teachings of parents and from the influence of faithful loyal friends.

A "far country" can be a desire to "be our own person and do our own thing" regardless of whom it hurts. Or it could be pride, temper, and/or lethargy. Temptations to yield to outside pressures are strong whether at home or away.

Jesus teaches in this parable that we *can* come to our senses, leave our "far country" and return to our heavenly Father. He will run to meet us and restore us to the relationship of Father-child. If we are lost we can be found!

There is one instance when we are *urged* to lose something, and in losing it we will find something greater. Jesus said: "He that loseth his life for my sake shall find it" (Matthew 10:39).

Faithfully Yours,
Farris

THINK ON THESE THINGS

1.   What is *your* definition of a parable?

2.   Jesus said, "I am the _____________ _____________"
     John 10:14.

3.   What value did Jesus place on a soul?

4.   Do you see a "working faith" on the part of the woman
     as she turned on the light and swept her house,
     diligently searching for her lost coin?

5.   Think of some "far countries" that can lure us.

6.   Discuss the father's action in giving the son his
     inheritance and allowing him to leave home.

7.   Do you see a parallel in this parable to God's allowing
     us to exercise our free will?   Does God force
     obedience?

8.   What should be the Christian's attitude toward one
     who is restored to his Father in heaven?

9.   Discuss the attitude of the elder brother in Luke
     15:25-32.

Chapter Eleven

Making the Bible Come Alive

For many years I have been encouraging those who sit in my classes to study God's Word. Yet many have told me they do not know how to study the Bible.

How can we make our Bible reading more exciting, more meaningful and more applicable to our lives?

Paul admonishes us in Colossians 3:16:

> Let the word of Christ dwell in you richly in all wisdom, teaching and admonishing one another . . .

God gave us His Word that it might *live* in us, abide in us, and be activated in our lives. God's Word is living and *active*.

> For the word of God is living and powerful, and sharper than any two-edged sword, piercing even to the division of soul and spirit, and of joints and marrow, and is a discerner of the thoughts and intents of the heart (Hebrews 4:12).

There is great joy in studying God's Word. Bible study is not an option. It is not something we can choose to do if and when we feel like it — not if we want to grow as a Christian. We are commanded by Holy Writ to "grow in the grace and knowledge of our Lord and Savior Jesus Christ" (2 Peter 3:18).

We need to be convinced of the need for Bible study. Why? Paul, writing to Timothy stated our need in simple language:

> All Scripture is given by inspiration of God, and is
> profitable for doctrine, for reproof, for correction, for
> instruction in righteousness, that the man of God may
> be complete, thoroughly equipped for every good work
> (2 Timothy 3:16,17).

Finding the time to study is difficult in our fast-paced world. Many obligations and responsibilities call to us. We are so busy — even "church work" crowds out time spent alone with God.

Bible study takes time, effort and concentration. Many of us are lazy Christians, not willing to give time and attention to studying. We offer many excuses for not studying, but most of them can be overcome through a renewed commitment to be all that God wants us to be.

The following guidelines will help us to become more dedicated students of His Word:

1. SET A TIME AND PLACE FOR DAILY BIBLE STUDY

The key word is *daily*. We take vitamins, but unless we take them daily they will do little good. The same is true of medication. The doctor insists we take our prescription pills daily. Otherwise we will not get well.

It seems strange we can find time for almost anything we want to do, but we cannot fit Bible reading time into our schedule. I am convinced time with God must become a conviction within. We must be absolutely devoted to growing in Christ.

A daily appointment with God should become a daily habit. Because of the diversity of our lives, each of us must find his or her own best time to meet with God.

Ideally, we need to purpose a time and place which can be kept on an on-going basis. We may not always be able to keep this time or be in this particular place, but setting a time and determining a place, will focus our minds and hearts. This is our *appointment with God*.

For some, this time may be early in the morning when most of us are the freshest and brightest. For others, the lunch break or just before bedtime seems to be the best time.

My time for Bible study is usually after breakfast. I need to have something on my stomach before I can fully concentrate. How eagerly I look forward to this time every morning!

> I rise before the dawning of the morn-
> ing, and cry for help; I hope in Your
> word (Psalm 119:147).

Thank God for His mornings! We can come to Him in prayer and find new hope and strength in His Word. We arise stronger and braver — more trusting somehow. We are ready to allow God to help us manage our communication with family and friends. We know He will give us wisdom as we ask for it. Morning by morning His promises seem more precious and true.

We need to deliberately plan this time even though interruptions are sure to come. People will need to see us. In the same way we are constantly making appointments with others. These appointments are duly marked on our calendars. We wouldn't think of breaking these appointments unless something comes up that seems more important.

We have an appointment with the King of Kings! When will we realize this is the most important engagement of our day? We should neglect other people before we neglect time with God.

It may mean taking the receiver off the hook, or going to a quiet place and closing the door. It may be necessary to let others know we have this appointment, and at the moment we cannot be disturbed. This time should be cherished. If we are too busy for God, we are simply *too* busy.

An hour of study may be too long, depending upon the circumstances. Fifteen minutes of quality time may be better than struggling an hour, all the while looking at our watches.

God deserves the best part of our day — when we are most alert. When our hearts are at their peak, we can come into His presence with joy and thanksgiving. We can't really give Him our best when we are tired and weary.

2. BEGIN WITH PRAYER

The best way to begin Bible study is with prayer. As we ask God's blessings on this time, He will be with us; guiding, helping, teaching.

Talking with God before we begin studying will prepare our hearts and minds to receive His truths. Psalm 119:18 should be the prayer of our lives and the beginning of our Bible study:

> Open my eyes, that I may see
> Wondrous things from Your law.

When we truly desire to find these "wondrous things," we will not stop reading until God helps us find them. He will open our eyes (open our hearts). He will assist us in paying attention. "Wondrous things" beyond imagination are found in His Word.

Sometimes we may get bogged down in such books as Ezekiel, Deuteronomy or the book of Revelation. It may be necessary to read a long time before we'll find wondrous things, but they are there! They are on every page.

3. APPROACH BIBLE STUDY WITH REVERENCE

The Bible is God's revealed Word — His personal love letter to each of us. A listening heart — a sense of wonder, will personalize these letters for us.

It will help us to remember God is speaking to us, as we *really* listen. He is talking to us as though He were speaking to a friend. He tells us the desires of His heart — He tells us how much He loves us, and gives us great and precious promises.

It is wonderful to know we can *hear* His precious voice speaking through His Word. Precious love letters! I used to look longingly for letters from my husband before we were married. I still long for letters from our children. God's Word should be even more cherished.

A sense of expectancy is paramount. We usually find that for which we are looking. If we are not hungry, we will not be fed. If we do not expect great truths to be revealed, we will gain little from our reading. It will not nourish or satisfy. We gain proportionally to what we have put into our study.

4. MARK YOUR BIBLES

I have marked four Bibles all the way through. I am presently marking the New King James Bible which my husband gave me for Christmas a few years ago.

Gazing at the clean white pages of my new Bible, I wondered which passage of Scripture to mark first. Opening my Bible, I decided to underline Philippians 3:10. It would become my goal for the new year:

> ... that I may know Him and the power
> of His resurrection, and the fellowship
> of His sufferings, being conformed to
> His death.

As I contemplated this verse, I was suddenly struck with the thought that I might have to suffer in order to participate in this knowing. "If this is what it takes," I prayed, "then let me suffer. I want to know Him better!" This brings us to our next point:

5. DESIRE TO KNOW GOD BETTER

We need to read God's Word in order to know Him better. I believe this should be our highest goal. Not just to know *about* Him, but to really *know* Jehovah God who created us, loved us, and gave us new life in Christ Jesus.

The best way to know God is through His Word. His nature, His purpose and His love are revealed on every page. God's Word changes us to the extent we allow God to work through His Word.

Let us discover everything we can about God, His Son, and the Holy Spirit. Discovering is a great adventure. The thoughts of men, as helpful as they may be, cannot take the place of making our own discoveries.

Discover the adventure and wonder of God Himself. He is mercifully kind, loving and compassionate. He holds all the answers to our problems. Every issue in life can be faced through a greater understanding of His Word.

The best definition of "discovering" is "finding something for the first time and putting it to use." We need to discover the remarkable power, presence and personality of God through the pages of His Book.

As we grow in Christ, this knowledge will not be merely external — it will come to live in our hearts by faith. Armed with faith, we then put the teachings of God into practice in our lives.

6. SEEK THE REVEALED WORD OF GOD. SEARCH AND FIND

It has often been said, "Seek and you will find. Search and be rewarded."

Jesus Himself, stated it most clearly in Matthew 7:7 and 8:

> Ask, and it will be given to you; seek,
> and you will find; knock, and it will be
> opened to you. For every one who asks
> receives, and he who seeks finds, and to
> him who knocks it will be opened.

I read about an American woman who traveled abroad to Sweden. While visiting in that country, she decided to learn the Swedish language. A devoted student of God's Word, she began reading the Swedish Bible.

One morning she was reading about the Berean Christians who "searched the Scriptures daily to find out whether these things were so," (Acts 17:11). To her surprise, she found that the Swedish word for "search" was rendered "ransack" in English.

Ransack is a very interesting word, meaning to search up and down, from right to left, high and low, and in all the by-places and corners. It means to "leave no stone unturned," so to speak.

It means to search with the intent to *find* that for which we are seeking. Are we searching with as much intensity as those who seek for gold, silver or precious things?

> And if you look for it as for silver and
> search for it as for hidden treasure, then
> you will understand the fear of the Lord
> (Proverbs 2:4,5). (NIV)

God's Word is like a deep mine, and we, like miners, search for treasures which need to be brought to the surface. The Word of God is filled and overflowing with precious treasures. Only as we dig, examine, probe, compare, and search diligently will they be found. We shall never discover buried treasures as long as we read with a lazy, half-hearted attitude. Jesus told us in Matthew 6:33:

> But seek first the kingdom of God and
> His righteousness, and all these things
> shall be added to you.

I cannot imagine anyone who has a sincere desire in "seeking first the kingdom of God" missing the joy of Bible study.

The perplexities of life often defeat us unless we allow God's messages to conquer our fears. Daily searching from the Bible will keep our hearts steadfast and sure, and our souls anchored in hope as the writer of Hebrews reveals in Hebrews 6:19:

> This hope we have as an anchor of the soul, both sure and steadfast, and which enters the Presence behind the veil.

A great promise is found in Jeremiah 29:12-14:

> Then you will call upon me and go and pray to Me, and I will listen to you. And you will seek Me and find Me, when you search for Me with all your heart. I will be found by you, says the Lord, and I will bring you back from your captivity.

We have learned that searching involves effort and exertion. We must then conclude that Bible *study* is essential to finding. There is a difference between reading and studying. Much of our time spent in God's Word is reading, and that is fine. But studying requires digging, looking underneath, examining from every angle, and exploring. To gain real meaning and understanding, one must learn the joy of diligent study.

We need to develop a *love* for Bible study. Do you remember your school days? On the occasions when you merely read your assignments, what happened? You were not prepared for the exams, were you?

You had to concentrate, commit the facts to memory and go over and over the assignment before you came to school on examination day. Remember the story about the elderly lady who was asked why she read her Bible so much? She replied: "Of course I am reading as much as I can. I am preparing for my final examinations!"

God's Word is simple in its admonitions: "Study to show yourselves approved..." (2 Timothy 2:15). (KJV)

7. LEARN TO MEDITATE UPON AND MEMORIZE SCRIPTURES

Why is it helpful to meditate upon the Scriptures daily? Why is memorization so needful? Because something stored is something deposited and kept. We are commanded by Holy Writ to store or lay up His Word in our hearts:

> Your word I have hidden in my heart,
> That I might not sin against you
> (Psalm 119:11).

Time spent in memorizing God's Word will pay more dividends than any other investment. We may deposit thousands of dollars in the bank and that bank may go bankrupt. We may invest in a "sure thing" only to find the investment has failed. There is only one investment which never fails — God's Word:

> Heaven and earth will pass away, but
> My words will by no means pass away
> (Mark 13:31).

I was impressed with the power of memorization as I read about the prisoners of war in Vietnam. Whenever their imprisonment became unbearable, they would share favorite verses with one another. These verses had been stored long ago in their hearts. Thus they were enabled to withdraw them at this critical period in their lives. They encouraged each other's faith and retained their own sanity as a result of repeating aloud verses once memorized and loved. The *Word* sustained and kept hope alive.

I am convinced one of the greatest things we can do for ourselves is to memorize Scripture. We can meditate on Scripture throughout the day only if we think about and have it in our minds. A determined effort to go over and over the words in our mind will reinforce not only the words themselves but the meaning of the words which is the purpose of memorization in the first place.

An unknown writer has given the following steps in memorization:

1. Read out loud a portion of the passage. Pick a portion which can be retained in the mind.
2. Read it out loud three times.
3. Then look up and say it out loud without looking three times.
4. Do the above once per day for four or five days.
5. On the fifth day try to join the portions together. Then read the whole verse three times, and then look up and say it three times.
6. Repeat this for a couple of days.
7. At the end of seven days merely read the passage once, then look up and say it once. You should have the passage memorized.
8. Go over the passage every two or three weeks so you will not forget it.

Jesus used the Word to combat Satan in the 4th chapter of Matthew when He said:

> It is written, man shall not live by bread
> alone, but by every word that proceeds
> from the mouth of God (Matthew 4:4).

Someone has wisely written these challenging words:

> Memorizing Scripture allows God's truth to gain more than just a toehold on our lives. It can be a catalyst for change, comfort and growth. It is like building a spiritual bank account with interest compounded daily. Most Christians believe in the value of a spiritual bank of memorized Scripture, but few make regular deposits.

> — Author Unknown

One morning I spent some time meditating and thinking about the following verse which is found in Isaiah 41:10:

> Fear not, for I am with you;
> Be not dismayed, for I am your God.
> I will strengthen you,
> Yes, I will help you,
> I will uphold you with My
> righteous right hand.

Approximately one hour after committing the above Scripture to memory, I had a "dismaying" experience. I had been working for days on this chapter, "storing" it in the *memory* of my word processor. I had finally revised it, polished it, ran a spelling check, and gave a sign of relief as I began printing the pages.

On the fourth page, the ribbon ran out. I knew I must replace it with a new one before I could proceed. Unfortunately, I am still learning the amazing mechanics of my word processor. Instead of consulting the manual, I turned the machine off!

After replacing the ribbon, I tried to call the manuscript back, only to discover that I had erased the entire work! Try as I might, I could not recall it, though I spent an hour trying to do so. It was lost, gone forever.

I sat at my desk, head bent, frustrated and disappointed beyond measure. All my work and effort wasted and lost! Then into my heart and mind came the words from God which I had memorized that morning! No longer did this seem a terrible loss. God was with me, He was giving me strength, helping me and upholding me with His "righteous right hand."

Now I am at work revising and rewriting. God's Word is marvelous in its application to the human experience. Two passages of Scripture come to mind:

> This is my comfort in my affliction,
> For Your word has given me life (Psalm
> 119:50).

And the wonderful consolation:

> So shall My word be that goes forth from My
> mouth; It shall not return to Me void, But
> it shall accomplish what I please, And it
> shall prosper in the thing for which I sent
> it (Isaiah 55:11).

8. KEEP BIBLE STUDY SIMPLE

Bible study is only complicated if we make it so. Many times we simply can't get started. It's hard for us to make the attempt. We think there must be a special place for us to begin. Just start reading! Reading in the Gospels is probably the best place to begin.

In case we have not been accustomed to reading the Bible, we need to begin with the "milk of the word." Leave the "meat" until later. We read in 1 Peter 2:2 and 3:

> . . . as newborn babes, desire the pure
> milk of the word, that you may grow
> thereby, if indeed you have tasted that
> the Lord is gracious.

In order for any of us to grow, we must eat. A baby deprived of milk will not grow; he will lose weight and physically deteriorate. In like manner, we will deteriorate spiritually should we be deprived of the nurture of God's teachings.

Keeping Bible study simple (at first) causes us to "grow in the grace and knowledge of our Lord and Savior Jesus Christ" at our own pace. Not everyone has the same capacity for growth. Reading difficult passages at first may cause us to be discouraged and can cause premature burnout.

Psalm 19:7 creates a spiritual thirst:

> The law of the Lord is perfect, convert-
> ing the soul; The testimony of the Lord
> is sure, making wise the simple.

Wisdom comes gradually and progressively, little by little, as we learn to digest through regular feedings. Let us not rush the process, but through continuous application of the Word, we will become mature and quite able to handle the "meat" of the Word.

9. LEARN TO CONCENTRATE

Learning to concentrate can become one of our greatest accomplishments in Bible study. We need to learn to pay attention to what we are reading. Inattentiveness comes about when we allow our minds to wander. We all know how hard it is to concentrate when we are over-tired or have too much on our minds. Little worries and cares can take their toll on concentration abilities.

As women we have many responsibilities. We have a thousand concerns and demands upon us daily. These responsibilities can get the best of us if we allow them to do so.

Since we as God's servants are so busy "going about doing good" it is well that we learn to concentrate in order to gain as much as we can from the limited time we spend in studying the Word.

I'd like to suggest that it is better to concentrate on one verse of Scripture, one thought or one passage, than it is to read whole para-graphs or chapters without gaining the meaning.

The writer of Hebrews states:

> Therefore we must give the more ear-
> nest heed to the things we have heard,
> lest we drift away (Hebrews 2:1).

Giving the "more earnest heed" to a verse demands concentration and effort. How much of our Bible study is "earnestly heeding?" Why are we to pay attention and take heed? "Lest we drift away!" We have all known friends who have drifted away because they have forsaken prayer, Bible study and church attendance. Let us not follow their example.

It is not unusual to get bogged down in Bible study. Perhaps we need to examine ourselves regularly to find the reasons for our indifference. God's Word is meant to be a shining beacon in a dark world. We are to study to show ourselves *approved*.

The passage found in 2 Timothy 2:15 which exhorts us to "study" (give diligence) to "show" (present) "thyself approved unto God, a workman that needeth not to be ashamed" (KJV) is worth a concentrated study in itself.

The words "approved unto God" mean "to prove by testing." God tests us through Bible study! The word "workman" in the Greek is also highly interesting. "Ergates" translates as "worker or laborer" in the New Testament. This points to the "work or labor" which is characteristic of diligent Bible study.

The most interesting phrase used in this Scripture is undoubtedly "rightly dividing" (handling aright). The original word for "dividing" which is "orthotomeo" means "to cut straight or evenly." Paul may have borrowed the idea from his experience in cutting the rough material he undoubtedly used in making tents. As an experienced tent maker he went to great pains to cut the material straight and even.

As students of God's Word, we are "to cut evenly through" the Scriptures and present them truthfully and honestly (straight forward) to others.

10. EXAMINE YOUR ATTITUDES

Why do we study the Bible? Have you ever asked yourself that question? Is it because we need to meet a daily program? Have we made a commitment to reading a chapter every day? We may have placed the Bible on a table beside our bed. At close of day, we reach for the Bible, which has been marked at the place we left off the day before. I would never discourage anyone from this habit, for I have often done this myself. Yet we need to understand our motives, our goals and attitudes.

Do we wish to read the Bible to prove a point or to satisfy our curiosity? God wants us to read His Word to grow, to know Him better and to show Him our love.

In her book *God's Joyful Surprise*, Sue Monk Kidd writes:

> When we search the Scriptures, for what are we really searching? An insight, some advice, a guiding principle? On the surface, yes. But maybe beneath all of that we are searching for God, for intimate encounter, for His love and presence in the midst of our daily lives. We want to connect with a Person, to become more at home with Him.

We need to pray for understanding, humility and obedience as we read. Obedient children do not question their father. They simply wish to please him.

WHERE IS YOUR BIBLE?

Children, where is your Bible,
*   When did you see it last?*
Since you sat and scanned its pages,
*   Say, how many days have passed?*

You have read your daily papers,
*   And with novels regaled yourself;*
But when did you read your Bible,
*   That lies untouched on the shelf?*

Christian, where is your Bible?
*   What is the place that you give*
To the book you say is your hope in death,
*   And that teaches you how to live?*

Don't say that your life is too busy;
*   Full many a soul is dead*
Because the book of eternal life,
*   Lies somewhere, unused, unread.*

— Author Unknown

11. BE CONSISTENT IN PRAISE AND PRAYER

As we read the Word of God, it should prompt us to praise and thank Him for all He has done for us. Psalm 119:4-7 spells out the reasons we cannot refrain from praising Him:

> You have commanded us to keep Your precepts
>   diligently.
> Oh, that my ways were directed to keep Your
>   *statutes!*
> Then I would not be ashamed, When I look into
>   all Your commandments.
> I will praise You with uprightness of heart,
>   When I learn
> Your righteous judgments.

Praise is certainly more than thanksgiving, but thanksgiving always includes praise. As we read His righteous judgments, we become saturated with the need to praise Him.

I believe our lives as women will be richer, sweeter, purer and deeper as we cultivate praise and gratitude. We need to have thankful hearts as we sit at the fountainhead of His outpouring love as expressed in the Bible.

While reading His Words we can also be praising Him at the same time:

> "Thank You, Father, for making this passage clear to
>   me."
> "Thank You , Lord, for changing my perspective about
>   this idea."
> "Father, You are so good to give me this passage of
>   Scripture. It is just what my heart needs!"
> "Lord, I was wrong. Now, I see my stubborn will has
>   been keeping me from doing what is right. Thank
>   You for pointing this out to me; convicting and
>   rebuking me."

Earthly fathers give us treasured truths and advice. Don't we wish to thank them? Our heavenly Father gives abundant treasures — so much so that we cannot begin to number them. We cannot thank Him enough for His wonderful blessings.

Praising Him for all His mercies and even the words of His mouth, will do wonders for our spirits. It will cause us to "humble ourselves in the sight of the Lord." As we"draw near to God" through the reading of the Bible, we will find "He will draw near to us." (James 4:8).

TRYSTING PLACE

My God and I have a trysting place
Here by my morning window
We meet together
Just He and I
In sweetness, gladness and praise.
I open His Word and Lo He appears
Blessing the rooms of my heart . . .
He sends morning
He sends day
He gives me high hopes
And my cares are all wiped away.

— Judy Miller

12. USE YOUR IMAGINATION. PRETEND YOU ARE THERE!

This is one of the most exciting, interesting experiences one can have. Pretend you are there! Pretend you are wearing the clothes the ladies might have been wearing then. Pretend you are feeling the sand between your toes as you walk the dusty roads. Can you savor the odor of bread being cooked over the coals?

Do you smell the scent of the sea? Can you hear the sound of the waves lapping over one another as you stand near the Sea of Galilee?

How would you feel if you were there, supposing Jesus was talking directly to you? Would you feel stronger and more capable of withstanding temptation than the people of those days? Would you respond to Christ with love and obedience supposing you were there?

Use your imagination. Go back in time — then realize Christ is as real and present today, as He was when He was on earth, walking the shores of Galilee and the streets of Nazareth. Everything in the Bible is for our learning. A sense of imagination will heighten our awareness.

13. MAKE YOURSELF READ

Some days we just don't feel like reading. We are either sick, worn out or discouraged. We allow our moods to influence us, therefore discouraging us so much, we want nothing more than to "throw in the towel." These are the days we need to read the most.

"I can't concentrate" we admit honestly. True, we can't . . . but we still have need of His presence. We can only find Him as we *think* of Him. Open up the Psalms on days we do not feel like praising the Lord. Allow the Psalmist to praise the Lord for us. Pretty soon, we'll find ourselves doing the same.

The Scriptures will lift our souls, enrich our hearts and soften our spirits. Many times, depending upon the circumstances, Bible reading will chase away the blues. How helpful it is to see things from God's viewpoint. Many times we look at situations from our own perspective. Our viewpoints can be so shallow; His, so deep. His ways are much higher than ours.

14. AVOID GETTING IN A RUT

The following concepts are a few examples of ways we can avoid getting into a rut as we read the Bible daily:

1. Approach your reading with a fresh viewpoint daily.
2. Try to imagine you are reading this passage for the first time.
3. Enjoy discovering new ideas, new concepts, new lessons.
4. Pray along with the Scriptures. Never forget He is present. Talk to the Lord about what you read.
5. Share what you read with others. Sharing with others reinforces the Scriptures in your own heart.
6. Allow the Word to motivate you to win souls. God wants us to go forth "bearing precious seed." The seed is His Word!
7. Keep a notebook of your studies. Write down what this passage means to you. Also write the passage in your own words.
8. Guard carefully against any distractions which rob you of your daily appointment with God.
9. Compose yourself when you come to read the Word. "Be still and know that I am God" (Psalm 46:10).
10. Do not rush through this time. Never should we rush in and out of His presence. 2 Corinthians 3:18 reminds us we need to take time to *behold* Him. Unless we take time to behold Him, we'll never be like Him.

How is your time with God? Is your Bible reading becoming more and more precious to you? Has the Bible come alive in your daily life?

The more time we spend with God the more teachable we will become. The Bible is a timeless book. It reaches us where we are. Nothing causes us to take stock of our lives as much as time spent in God's Word.

15. LAST OF ALL, OBEY THE TRUTHS JUST DISCOVERED

James 1:22 says "But be doers of the word, and not hearers only, deceiving yourselves." If we do not put into practice what we have learned, it will be head-knowledge only. It will be like looking into a mirror and forgetting what kind of person we are (James 1:24).

Way back in the Old Testament God convinced Ezekiel that His words were falling on deaf and indifferent ears. Yes, the people came to listen to him speak the prophecies he had received from God, but they paid no attention. They admired the way Ezekiel spoke the words; they thought he had a beautiful way of expressing himself. But that was as far as it went. No action was taken in response to His teaching:

> As for you, son of man, the children of your people are talking about you beside the walls and in the doors of the houses; and they speak to one another, everyone saying to his brother, 'Please come and hear what the word is that comes from the Lord.'

> So they come to you as people do, they sit before you as My people, and they hear your words, but they do not do them; for with their mouth they show much love, but their hearts pursue their own gain.

> Indeed you are to them as a very lovely song of one who has a pleasant voice and can play well on an instrument; for they hear your words, but they do not do them (Ezekiel 33:30-32).

The more we act upon the knowledge we have received, the stronger Christians we shall become. Through Bible study we will gain victorious living. Heaven is our portion. Let us keep our eyes on the goal.

Blessed is he who reads and those who
hear the words of this prophecy, and
keeps those things which are written in
it; for the time is near (Revelation 1:3).

**Faithfully Yours,
Judy**

THINK ON THESE THINGS

1. God gave us His Word that it might _______ in us,_______in us and be ___________________ in our lives.

2. Why don't we read the Bible more?

3. A daily appointment with God should become a _______ __________ .

4. What is the best way to begin Bible Study?

5. How should we approach Bible study?

6. Why is it helpful to mark our Bibles?

7. True or false? One reason to study our Bibles is to know more about God?

8. We can compare God's Word to a _______ _______. We can compare outselves to _____________.

9. Searching our Bible requires ________ and _________ .

10. Why is it helpful to meditate upon the Scriptures daily?

12. What is one of our greatest accomplishments in Bible study?

13. What does it mean to be "approved unto God?"

14. Name some ways we can avoid getting into ruts as we study the Bible.

Chapter Twelve

What Manner of Life ?

"Therefore, since all these things will be dissolved, what manner of persons ought you to be in holy conduct and godliness" (2 Peter 3:11).

God has called us to press toward the mark of the upward call in Jesus Christ. This is the high and noble theme of our lives. Let us consider three important questions that will help us to press on:

IN VIEW OF THE FACT THAT WE HAVE A SINFUL NATURE, WHAT MANNER OF LIFE OUGHT WE TO LIVE?

The setting for our study is set in the 33rd chapter of Ezekiel. The book of Ezekiel challenges us to dig deep. Chapter 33 is a message applicable not only to the children of Israel, but to us today as well.

All ancient cities were fortified with a protecting wall which surrounded the entire city. As a means of defense, the wall protected the city from the attacking forces of the enemy.

These enemies often set themselves against God's people. Inside the wall was a high tower where sentinels guarded the fortress.

In that territory, a watchman was appointed. His job was to warn the people when he observed that an enemy was approaching.

Ezekiel, already God's prophet, received a new commission from God:

> . . . son of man: I have made you a watchman for the house of Israel; therefore you shall hear a word from My mouth and warn them for Me (Ezekiel 33:7).

Ezekiel's new commission was to warn the people. How was he to do this?

He was to warn the people by blowing a trumpet. At the sound of the trumpet the people would know the enemy was coming. The trumpet was sounded as a signal — a warning signal to alert God's people.

God said:

> Then whoever hears the sound of the trumpet and does not take warning, if the sword comes and takes him away, his blood shall be on his own head. He heard the sound of the trumpet, but did not take warning; his blood shall be upon himself. But he who takes warning will save his life (verses 4 and 5).

In other words, once the people heard the sound of the trumpet, knew the enemy was coming, yet did not pay attention — then his life was in his own hands. He was responsible and would die in his own iniquity.

We also notice a warning is given to the watchman:

> But if the watchman sees the sword coming and does not blow the trumpet, and the people are not warned, and the sword comes and takes any person from among them, he is taken away in his iniquity, but his blood I will require at the watchman's hands (verse 6).

If the watchman did not blow the trumpet as God had instructed, then the blood of the people was upon *him*. He was responsible for warning the people by blowing the trumpet.

What happened if he did not sound the warning? God took the life of the watchman and allowed the enemy to take the life of the people. Remember, though, the blood of the people was on the watchman's hands.

> When I say to the wicked, 'O wicked man, you shall surely die!' and you do not speak to warn the wicked from his way, that wicked man shall die in his iniquity, but his blood I will require at your hand. Nevertheless if you warn the wicked to turn from his way, and he does not turn from his way, he shall die in his iniquity; but you have delivered your soul (verses 8 and 9).

If the watchman obeyed God and warned the people, and they still did not respond, the prophet was not responsible. God promised him that his soul would be delivered.

God then told Ezekiel to speak to the people because they were asking questions:

> If our transgressions and our sins lie
> upon us, and we pine away in them,
> *how can we then live?* (verse 10,
> emphasis mine).

Good question! In other words, "If we are going to die in our sins, what do our lives mean to us? If you are going to reject us, O God, and punish us for not heeding Your warnings, what purpose is there in living?

Then Ezekiel was instructed to say to the people:

> As I live, says the Lord God, I have no
> pleasure in the death of the wicked, but
> that the wicked may turn from his way
> and *live*. Turn, turn from your evil
> ways! For why should you die, O house
> of Israel? (verse 11, emphasis mine).

All the way through the Old Testament, God emphasizes the fact that he wants his children to *live,* really live! And He spells out the definition of *life.* The following is one of my favorite passages from Deuteronomy 30:19,20:

> I have set before you life and death,
> blessing and cursing; therefore choose
> life, that both you and your descen-
> dants may live; that you may love the
> Lord your God, that you may obey His
> voice, and that you may cling to Him,
> for He is your life and the length of
> your days (Deuteronomy 30:19 and 20).

God, through His Son, Jesus Christ, has given us "all things that pertain to life and godliness" (2 Peter 1:3). Everything we need for a happy, fulfilling life is found in following God's commandments and keeping ourselves in the love of Christ. Jesus, Himself, spoke these enthralling words:

> I have come that they may have life, and
> that they may have it more abundantly
> (John 10:10).

To merely exist is not living; but abiding in Christ brings us abundant life. In his commentary on John, William Barclay writes:

> The Greek phrase used for *having it more abundantly* means to have a *superabundance of a thing*. To be a follower of Jesus, to know who He is and what He means, is to have a superabundance of life. A Roman soldier came to Julius Caesar with a request for permission to commit suicide. He was a wretched dispirited creature with no vitality. Caesar looked at him. "Man," he said, "were you ever really alive?" When we try to live our own lives, life is a dull dispirited thing. When we walk with Jesus, there comes a new vitality, and superabundance of life. It is only when we live with Christ that life becomes really worth living and we begin to live in the real sense of the word.

IN VIEW OF THE FACT THAT ALL OF THESE THINGS ARE GOING TO BE DISSOLVED, WHAT MANNER OF LIFE OUGHT WE TO LIVE?

Our setting is now in the third chapter of 2nd Peter. Verse 10 describes a watchman's warning:

> But the day of the Lord will come as a
> thief in the night, in which the heavens
> will pass away with a great noise, and
> the elements will melt with fervent
> heat; both the earth and the works that
> are in it will be burned up.

Peter stands here in the place of a watchman. God, through the Holy Spirit, has instructed him to warn the people of what is someday going to come to pass. The above Scripture is a future tense verse which we all need to take to heart. Someday the heavens are going to pass away with a great noise.

That great noise is the noise of fire. We have all heard the roar of a huge fire. It is a terrifying sound. All the heavens (atmosphere) will pass away, and the earth will melt with fervent heat. A scorching, red-hot, boiling heat would better describe this kind of heat. There is no doubt that this world is going to perish and be destroyed by fire some day.

Several years ago our youngest daughter, Susan, and I were watching a documentary on TV. The demolition of a 20-story building took place before our very eyes.

The demolition expert pulled a lever on a machine, and the entire building crumbled like a tiny toy. Smoke and flames billowed up. After the smoke cleared away, nothing was left but a heap of rubbish. The embers and flames burned low; everything was destroyed in a moment, in the twinkling of an eye.

The same thing will happen at the end of time — it will occur all over the world. The things we are buying and laying up on earth are not going to last — they are going to be totally burned up and destroyed. This motivates us to place our treasures in heaven.

What kind of lives are Christians to live since we know these things are going to happen? Are we going to be burned up along with all the elements?

Paul gets right to the heart of the matter when he tells Christians not to "sorrow as others who have no hope" (1 Thessalonians 4:13). Then he continues with these great words of consolation and hope:

> For the Lord Himself will descend from heaven with a shout, with the voice of an archangel, and with the trumpet of God. And the dead in Christ will rise first. Then we who are alive and remain shall be caught up together with them in the clouds to meet the Lord in the air. And thus we shall always be with the Lord. Therefore comfort one another with these words (verses 16-18).

The question you and I must answer is, "What manner of life" shall we live while we are waiting for these things to come to pass? What shall be our attitude?

Let us look closer at the text in 2 Peter 3:

> Verse 11: "in holy conduct and
> godliness"
> Verse 12: "looking for and hastening
> the coming of the day of God"
> Verse 13: "Look for new heavens and a
> new earth"
> Verse 14: "be diligent to be found by
> Him in peace."
> Verse 14: "without spot and blameless"
> Verse 17: "beware lest you also fall
> from your own steadfastness"
> Verse 18: " . . . grow in the grace and
> knowledge of our Lord and Savior
> Jesus Christ"

In verse 11, Peter calls to our attention that we are to watch our conduct. It is to be a conduct which is characterized by holiness and godliness.

Are our lives holy? Is our conduct godly? Are we living righteous, pure and godly lives? We are to live expectantly with this kind of daily conduct.

GODLINESS

My definition for godliness is "devotion to God." A woman who is godly is a woman devoted to God! Her whole life is centered in God. She has come to the point in life where nothing matters except her life in God. Her life is "hidden with Christ in God" (Colossians 3:3).

She has set her *affections* on God, which is another term for "devotion." Her heart is set on "things above, not on things on the earth." She knows "Christ is sitting at the right hand of God" (Colossians 3:1) and that's where she longs to be also. She is like Paul who said, "It is no longer I who live, but Christ lives in me" (Galatians 2:20).

A godly woman is a person who is "dead" to this world; one who is striving to put to death the lusts and passions of the flesh. She is happy whether she lives or dies, for like Paul, she can say, "For to me, to live is Christ, and to die is gain" (Philippians 1:21).

She is a woman who, apart from God, would be empty and floundering around in this world. With God she is complete. She knows why she was born, the reason she is here, and where she is going.

A traveler once asked Socrates "How can I reach Mt. Olympus?"

He replied, "Just make every step you take go in that direction."

The Christian woman's trust, belief and love for God in Christ Jesus has given her life meaning and direction. She takes every step "in that direction."

She has made a commitment. It is as strong as Paul's when he wrote to Timothy:

> . . . for I know whom I have believed
> and am persuaded that He is able to
> keep what I have committed to Him
> until that Day (2 Timothy 1:12).

She has come to be filled with the fullness of God, which is so satisfying and sufficient that she knows it passes all understanding and knowledge. (Ephesians 3:19). It is something so precious and sweet, she would not exchange it for anything in this world.

What is the outward manifestation of a godly woman?

Her quiet, serene manner shows through her eyes, smile, manner, behavior, speech, posture, poise and demeanor. It shows in her service, her interests, her pleasures, her relationships and her church attendance. It shows in her dress, her appearance and even the way she walks and talks.

> Do not let your beauty be that outward
> adorning of arranging the hair, of
> wearing gold, or of putting on fine
> apparel; but let it be the hidden person
> of the heart, with the incorruptible
> ornament of a gentle and quiet spirit,
> which is very precious in the sight of
> God. For in this manner, in former
> times, the holy women who trusted in
> God also adorned themselves, being
> submissive to their own husbands (1
> Peter 3:3-5).

IN VIEW OF GOD'S TRANSFORMING LOVE WHAT MANNER OF LIFE OUGHT WE TO LIVE?

Ezekiel 16 is a chapter about God's redeeming grace, mercy and love set against the backdrop of Israel's rebellious spirit.

Time and again, Israel rebelled against God. God called them a stubborn stiff-necked people. God's transforming love brought them back to their original relationship.

When I was a little girl I used to love reading fairy stories. One of my favorites was the story of the handsome prince who, through an evil spell, had been changed into an ugly, despicable, disgusting, revolting frog.

The only way he could be transformed into the handsome prince again, was if someone with enough love and compassion would come along and kiss the ugly, despicable, disgusting, revolting frog.

Sure enough, a beautiful princess came along and fell in love with him. She kissed him, and with that kiss he was changed back into the handsome prince again.

Do you remember the story of *My Fair Lady?* That plot involved Professor Higgins who made a bet with a friend that he could take a plain, ordinary girl off the streets and turn her into a beautiful lady.

He chose Eliza, who was very impulsive and frivolous. Little by little, he taught her how to walk, how to use proper table utensils, how to dress and fix her hair, and most of all he taught her proper elocution.

After all these lessons, she was transformed into a beautiful young woman who could talk with other ladies in the finest places. Professor Higgins loved her enough to spend time refining her life.

Ezekiel 16 describes God's great transforming love. The nation of Israel, God's chosen people, is compared to new born babies. This is an analogy which is easy to understand:

> As for your nativity, on the day you were born, your navel cord was not cut, nor were you washed in water to cleanse you; you were not rubbed with salt nor swathed in swaddling clothes. No eye pitied you, to do any of these things to you, to have compassion on you; but you were thrown out into the open field, when you yourself were loathed on the day you were born (Ezekiel 16:4 and 5).

Here we see a pitiful picture of the Israelite nation. They were hated and despised and thrown out into the open field. Picture it! Their navel cords were not cut, birth blood was still dripping down. They were not rubbed with salt, which means they were not properly cleansed. They were not wrapped in swaddling clothes . . . long strips of cloth which were wrapped around the babies like little mummies.

No one cared anything about them . . . no one had any compassion for them. They were thrown out on a rubbish heap; left there to die.

This presents a picture of the human condition. We, too, were left out in the field, so to speak, to die in our sins. Had not Christ come along, giving His life, shedding His blood on the cross, we would still be there struggling for our lives.

Struggling! Yes, all of us were struggling in our own blood, waiting for someone to come to our rescue.

> But God demonstrates His own love
> toward us, in that while we were still
> sinners, Christ died for us   (Romans
> 5:8).

The good hand of God has always been upon His people to rescue us and buy us back, "while we were still sinners."

In the 6th verse of the 16th chapter of Ezekiel we see the saving power of God as He reaches down to redeem mankind:

> And when I passed by you and saw you
> struggling in your own blood, I said to
> you in your blood, "live!" Yes, I said to
> you in your blood, "live!"

God came along and rescued those little infants on the rubbish heap, tossed out in the open field. He held them close to His breast and saved them from eternal death. Not only did He save them, He made them thrive!

> I made you thrive like a plant in the
> field; and you grew, matured, and
> became very beautiful. Your breasts
> were formed, your hair grew, but you
> were naked and bare (Ezekiel 16:7).

"You were naked and bare." Yes, all of us were spiritually "naked and bare," empty without God in our lives. We needed Someone who would rescue us from the rubbish heap. Verse 8 is one of the most redemptive verses in all God's Word:

> When I passed by you again and looked upon you, indeed your time was the time of love; so I spread My wing over you and covered your nakedness. Yes, I swore an oath to you and entered into a covenant with you, and you became Mine," says the Lord God.

Does this verse cause gratitude to well up in you? God says to you and me, "I spread My wing over you and covered your nakedness."

Here we see a beautiful wedding custom. The bridegroom lovingly escorts his bride to his chamber. He takes off his outer cloak, spreads it over his bride, covering her nakedness. In that act, they become one. "I am going to protect you, watch over you, and warm you with my love" was symbolized in this one redemptive act.

"I . . . entered into a covenant with you, and you became Mine." These are the words of a royal bridegroom spoken to his bride. And isn't the Church *His* bride? (Revelation 21:2).

The Church is described as a bride adorned in "fine linen, clean and bright" in Revelation 19:8. A bride is supposed to be ready for her bridegroom when he comes.

> Let us be glad and rejoice and give Him glory, for the marriage of the Lamb has come, and His wife has made herself ready (Revelation 19:7).

God also has sworn to us in Ezekiel 16:8 that He has entered into a covenant with us. The word *covenant* is such a wonderful word. It signifies God's agreement and promise to us, and ours to Him. We must never forget our side of the agreement. We tell God "I will love You, serve You, honor and obey You. I promise You; this is my covenant with You." Doesn't this sound like a wedding vow? A wedding vow is meant to be kept forever and ever.

The Lord, then, says to His bride, "And you became Mine." I praise the Lord for these words. I am not meant to live alone. I do not belong to myself; I belong to God and He belongs to me.

The narrative goes on to describe how He dresses and adorns His bride. He gives her many wonderful gifts, but the finest of all is the beautiful crown which He places on her head. (verse 12). The King has made her His queen!

At the close of verse 13, we read these words:

> You were exceedingly beautiful, and
> succeeded to royalty.

Where had she originated? Where had the King found her? She was found in the open field, tossed upon a garbage heap, left there to die. But God snatched her from that terrible place, breathed spiritual life into her, and advanced her to royalty!

If only we could recognize down deep within our hearts that which God has done for each of us. If only we could remember our origins and what we were before He transformed us by His love. He touched each one of us with His love, took our brokenness and shame upon Him, and now we are no longer the same. He took us off a pile of rubbish, and binding the broken pieces, He put us back together again ... making us whole and complete in Him.

In verse 14, we find that our "beauty" is perfect through His splendor. God is continually perfecting us in holiness.

How shall we then live? Titus 3:3-7 gives us the answer:

> For we ourselves were also once fool-
> ish, disobedient, deceived, serving
> various lusts and pleasures, living in
> malice and envy, hateful and hating one
> another. But when the kindness and
> the love of God our Savior toward man
> appeared, not by works of righteous-
> ness which we have done, but
> according to His mercy He saved us,
> through the washing of regeneration
> and renewing of the Holy Spirit, whom
> He poured out on us abundantly
> through Jesus Christ our Savior, that
> having been justified by His grace we
> should become heirs according to the
> hope of eternal life.

IF YOU COULD HAVE ANOTHER LIFE

If you could have another life
To live,
What would you do
To make your own life bless the lives
Of those who follow you?

If you could have another life
To live,
Would you be kind,
And speak each word with other men's
Deep longings in your mind?

If you could live another life,
Would you
Be harsh and gruff,
And add a burden to a heart
Whose load was great enough?

If you could live another life,
Could you
Forget at all
To give cold water to a child
Whose loaf was stale, and small?

If you could have another life
To live, How would it go?
Would it be like yesterday?
Today? A week ago?

— Mary Oler

If you knew Christ were coming tomorrow, how would you live today?

Faithfully Yours,
Judy

THINK ON THESE THINGS

1. What was the purpose of ancient walls?

2. How was Ezekiel to warn the people?

3. What happened if he did not sound the warning?

4. What was the important question people were asking?

5. How will the day of the Lord come?

6. What is to be the character of the Christian's conduct?

7. What is the definition for godliness?

8. What is the outward manifestation of a godly woman?

9. Ezekiel 16 shows us God's ________________ ________________ _______ .

10. With what analogy did God describe the Israelite nation in Ezekiel 16?

11. Of what does the rubbish heap in the open field remind us?

12. What does "I spread my wing over you" mean?

13. What does the word *covenant* mean?

14. How has God transformed us by His love?

BIOGRAPHICAL SKETCHES OF THE AUTHORS

Farris Parker

Farris Parker and her husband of fifty-seven years have lived in Houston, Texas, since 1937, having moved from Hot Springs, Arkansas. She and "Hack" are members of the Southeast Church of Christ, Houston.

Both enjoy fishing, attending all the family "camp-outs," as well as other functions of the family ministry. Her hobbies are reading, gardening and handwork.

Farris (her friends call her "Fairy") has taught Ladies' Bible Classes for over 35 years; however her real love of teaching was the years she taught Junior and Senior high school girls. She has seen many of them develop into teachers, wives of elders, missionaries and preachers.

She has spoken on many Ladies' Day programs throughout Texas, and has conducted workshops for wives of non-Christians.

Farris is a fourth-generation Christian and has been a Christian for 63 years. She has taken seriously Paul's commandment in Titus 2:3-5:

> . . . the older women likewise,
> that they be reverent in behavior,
> not slanderers, not given to much
> wine, teachers of good things —
> that they admonish the young
> women to love their husbands, to
> love their children, to be discreet,
> chaste, homemakers, good, obe-
> dient to their own husbands, that
> the word of God may not be
> blasphemed.

Judy Miller

Judy Miller is the wife of Jule Miller, producer of the "Visualized Bible Series" filmstrips and videos. The Millers reside in Pasadena, Texas, and attend Southeast Church of Christ in Houston.

They have ten children and twenty-two grandchildren. All ten children are Christians, and two of the grandchildren, Joy and Matthew, have been baptized.

Judy has written eight previous books, the last being a study book entitled *Ripples on the Water*. Her hobbies are reading, teaching, writing, handwork, and caring for her grandchildren.

She speaks extensively across the nation for Ladies' Day Programs, retreats and university lectureships. Jule and Judy presently are spending much of their time conducting weekend Soul-Winning Workshops.

BIBLIOGRAPHY

Barclay, William. *The Gospel of John,* (Daily Study Bible Series). Philadelphia, Westminster Press, 1975.

Barnett, Joe. Excerpt from church bulletin.

Breck, Mrs. Frank A, and Tullar, Grant Colfax. "Face to Face," (hymn), *Songs of the Church,* A. H. Howard, ed., West Monroe, LA, Howard Publishing Co., 1975.

Carroll, Lewis. *Alice in Wonderland,* New York, A. L. Burt Co., n.d.

Douglas, Lloyd D. *The Robe,* Boston, Houghton Mifflin Co., 1942.

Dunn, David. *Try Giving Yourself Away,* Englewood Cliffs, NJ, Prentice-Hall, 1970.

Fulghum, Robert. *All I Really Need to Know I Learned in Kindergarten,* New York, Villard Books, 1989.

Horne, Donna. *Meanwhile, Back in the Jungle,* Winona, MS, J. C. Choate Publications.

Jones, Ruby. *Odds 'N' Ends,* (newspaper column), Daleville, Indiana.

Kidd, Sue Monk. *God's Joyful Surprise,* San Francisco, Harper and Row, 1987.

Mitchell, Ethelyn. *Come Unto Me,* Abilene, TX, Quality Printing Co., 1963.

Oxenham, John. *God's Sunshine,* (poem).

Shakespeare, William. *As You Like It,* Act II, Scene 7, Line 174.

Weatherhead, Leslie. *Christ Instead,* (poem).